I'M A BOSS, ...

I'M A BOSS NOT A SHRINK

PRACTICAL GUIDE TO MANAGER WELLBEING CONVERSATIONS

HEATHER BEACH

HEALTHYWORK
COMPANY
enabling thriving cultures

To my Mum and Dad who left so much love behind them.

To Rosie, Wendy, Richard, Maria and George ... and to the other Richard, Rosie's dad, for making life easier.

EXTRA RESOURCES

Test your own manager conversations skills with this quiz before you start the book:

https://imabossnotashrink.scoreapp.com

If you would like to work with Healthy Work Company, scan the QR code below or click the link to access our contact details:

https://healthyworkcompany.com/contact

CONTENTS

FOREWORD

by Lauren Applebey, Mental Health Lead at Meta

I have been lucky enough to have spent 17 years working in health, safety and wellbeing from construction sites, to transport, from prisons to high tech. Twelve of those years I spent working with Heather, or Beachy as I like to call her.

I think I am, therefore, the right person to set the scene – not just to let you know why this book will help you to become a more empathic manager, who not only sets better boundaries for yourself but is more self-aware and self-reflective – but who *role models* a better culture for corporate wellbeing.

As Heather demonstrates in this book, role modelling as managers is such a huge part of the permission people seek for balance. "I am popping to the gym after this meeting", "I worked late last night, so I'll start a little later tomorrow", "My children's sports day comes first". These words are like gold for a team member who is not sure if they can stop and take a break and reflect on their own balance.

As managers, we set the tone and the pace of work, we give people the room and safety to ask 'stupid questions', challenge negative behaviour and think outside of the box. We deliver the difficult messages, keep up the communication – and balance performance with wellbeing. As Heather lays out, *it is hard* – and we haven't necessarily been taught how to manage, or certainly how to manage people in a very complex world where expectations are high, and resources and capacity are often diminished.

For over a decade Heather was my manager. I actually followed her from one company to the next, twice! Did she always get it right? Probably not. Was she genuine, transparent and vulnerable? Absolutely.

The day I had my interview with Heather back in 2008, when I was only 23, was the day after one of my childhood school friends had tragically passed away from cancer. I sat in the car park outside the office in tears, before taking a deep breath and going into my interview. I really wanted this job. The interview was fine. I did OK. But I knew I was distracted and hardly the best version of myself.

The recruiter called with strange feedback. "Heather really liked you, but something wasn't right. She could see you weren't really there and that you could be so much better." I explained the situation to the recruiter. Heather invited me back, wiped the slate clean and we started over. I got the job, and it was the start of something that would become much bigger.

There have been many moments of serendipity that I have shared with Heather. When she started Healthy Work Company I was working as a freelance health and wellbeing writer and going through some pretty tough stuff personally, including a cancer scare which made me promise myself I would never say no to anything again (slightly stupid!). Not long after this over-the-top announcement to myself, I messaged Heather to wish her daughter a good first day at secondary school. She replied, "Come and work for me delivering mental health training." And I did – and I was pretty good at it. Heather saw something in me that I didn't see in myself.

We worked together for the next few years supporting big companies to create big mental health and wellbeing strategies. Travelling the length of the country each week, from the offices of ITV to Nestlé, from Astra Zeneca to Luton and Heathrow Airports, Serco to The Telegraph, delivering training from the boardroom to the shop floor. We never stopped at training, it was always about implementation and review, making a tangible difference – not ticking a box.

Heather brought her expertise of health, safety and wellbeing, coupled it with her understanding of culture and leadership, and was a leap ahead of those bringing in Pilates and cycle to work schemes. The key was to get businesses to focus on systemic psychological risk, preventative mental health management – and she always followed up every stat with a quote from another dead Greek philosopher, or shared new learnings from the world of academia.

Throughout all of this, she was my manager. And throughout my time at Healthy Work Company, I went through a divorce with two children impacted, two pregnancy losses with my new partner, and the devastating loss of my brother, Ali, who was due to become a father for the first time. Ali had worked with Healthy Work Company to help build our e-learning – Heather was one of the first people I told. Honestly, I don't remember much about the conversation but I just knew she was there, she was at his funeral and she allowed me to deal with my grief, my way.

Having lost my mum at eight, I was always told I didn't 'grieve well'. I was OK, and people didn't like that. People say it's "ok to not be ok". I say it's also "fine to be fine". I am someone who likes to carry on. I need to work. I need purpose and meaning, pressure and challenge. That is how humans thrive, and Heather explores that throughout these pages. I am determined to grow through hardship, to learn rather than survive. Heather checked in but gave me the space to get back to work at my own speed. I wanted to get back to the front of the room delivering training – because that is when I am in my flow – when nothing else exists.

What Heather did personally was always be honest about her own situation. This allowed me to do the same. She shared her own struggles, talked openly about the reality of life – no false pretence, no Instagram filter.

She was always to the point, maybe sometimes candid, maybe sometimes blunt – but there was no fluffiness and beating around the bush. She wasn't trying to fix my situation but supported me in navigating it. She would pick up on the signs that something wasn't right and ask the question. "You are not yourself at the moment. What's going on?"

What Heather has done in the world of corporate mental health is to shift the conversation from helping those who are ill (still an incredibly important part of the job) to supporting workforces to thrive *through* work, not despite it. She ensures that we don't throw more "stuff" at wellbeing but zoom out and reflect on the wider context.

I have taken so much from this and brought it to one of the world's biggest companies, where I now co-lead mental health strategy, resources and benefits. As you delve into the pages of this book, I hope you too will take away something really meaningful that changes the way you support your teams – not to give you more work to do, but actually to remind you where your role begins and ends. Because, after all – you're a boss, not a shrink.

PROLOGUE

Perfectionism is a twenty-ton shield that we lug around thinking it will protect us when, in fact, it's the thing that's really preventing us from taking flight.
Brené Brown

Back in 2017, I was approaching an important birthday and it wasn't 40. I had a great job running events, conferences and information services in the health and safety sector as a Director for a global business, but I felt an inexorable pull – one of those itches you simply can't ignore – to do my own thing.

I don't know where I found the courage, and having embarked on the roller coaster of running my own business, I am not sure I could do it again. But I resigned, re-mortgaged my house, started a master's degree in applied positive psychology, and held a launch conference, 'Mental health for health and safety professionals' where Alastair Campbell spoke about living with bipolar disorder.

I wanted to achieve two key things through Healthy Work Company. I wanted to help organisations take a strategic look at wellbeing as a business enabler. I also wanted to help solve one of the workplace challenges that I had really struggled with myself in my career as a manager and, later, as a manager of managers.

That problem, in 2017, was nowhere near as big as it is now! You might be familiar with it…

You are picking up signs that someone isn't themselves. Perhaps you've noticed that their performance is off, (perhaps, truth be told, you found yourself getting a bit irritated about that!) or they've become really quiet or snappy. You suspect they are struggling with something – you don't know if it's personal or work-related.

It might even be you that is giving them angst! (If so, you'd **really** rather not know!)

You want to be kind, but really you just hope it will go away…

And it might of course!

But it might also get worse. The individual might go off sick and then you can't contact them then because they'd think you were harassing them, right? (This is wrong by the way – but we will get into that in Chapter 14: D for your Duties as a manager.)

Perhaps their performance dips further and you start to move down a performance improvement plan or disciplinary process with them and then, of course, they get signed off sick.

Ultimately, they probably leave, or you exit them (which, by the time you get to that point you might actually feel relieved about!). And, hopefully you have managed it in such a way that they don't take the business to a tribunal….

Whatever transpires, there is disruption to the team, to you and to the individual. All that angst and eventually anger on both sides. The open job role, which if that person is off sick, you can't recruit for.

Why do we bury our heads in the sand when we first notice these things?

We might worry if it is our place, or even our business, to ask.

Is work really a place where emotions should be surfaced? If you do dare to start the conversation, you worry about:

- The person being angry and telling you where to go!
- Feeling like you are being intrusive
- What they might say (perhaps about you!)
- Not knowing what to say
- Saying the wrong thing
- Making it worse for the person
- Dealing with emotion (yours or theirs)

Most managers want to do the right thing. Whilst they may have a spectrum of ability to empathise, they don't aim to be unhelpful. However, they are balancing the needs of the business with the needs of the person and lots of them are very performance driven – that's how they got to the position they are in. There is always too much to do, and they might try to avoid a conversation which would open a further can of worms and which they don't ultimately know how to handle correctly.

This failure to act at a time before the problem becomes insurmountable is not only a business problem, but also a human one. As more businesses look to balance performance and care, as more of them at least speak good words about equity and inclusion, as collaboration and diversity are seen to become business enablers, managers simply **must** be trained to hold difficult conversations like this one.

In launching Healthy Work Company, the first thing I did was sit down with a brilliant Human Resources Employment lawyer, Pam Loch, and ask her to write a course with me to help managers with this particular conversation.

The first few courses we ran went into detail on the legal framework and on what could go wrong if you mismanaged it. As time went on, it became clear that people wanted best practice, and gradually I turned it into a simple ABCD-step process (aided by my associate at the time – Lauren Applebey, who now works as Mental Health Lead at Meta).

I have now worked with thousands of managers all over the world to train them in simple steps to having good conversations with someone who is struggling – we call it a 'manager wellbeing conversation'. We offer this both online and face to face. We have worked with organisations such as ITV, Eurostar, The Telegraph, Mace, Abel and Cole, Kuehne and Nagel to mention but a few. Over time, the training has changed and become more and more effective, dealing also with the increasing challenge of hybrid work, and often using actors in a forum theatre technique, where the audience coaches the actors to handle the conversation better. This is a safe way to examine a challenging conversation.

If you are interested in working with me, or my giving a talk to your organisation – just scan the QR code at the front of the book.

Are managers trained in management?

As an enthusiastic young spark, at the tender age of 23, I was promoted to management. This was my first job and it was with a leading-edge tech company called SilverPlatter. We were the first company to put full-text information on a CD-ROM and to deliver academic learning over the internet.

Informality ruled. It was a wonderful, crazy, creative place where lifelong friendships were forged, leadership experimented with, and we got the chance to learn on the job.

Yet we were moving from a small business to one growing globally at pace, necessitating the need for structure and process. We hired someone into our first HR role in my second year there. That was a shock to us all. That informal conversation, "It's not really working is it? Take a few weeks to find yourself another job and we will keep paying you until you do" was replaced with formal disciplinary and performance management processes.

In my role as a very young new manager, with direct reports who were all older than me, I received no training in how to manage people. I was expected to work it out.

Whilst this was 30 years ago now, things haven't changed that much. The UK Trade Union Council (TUC) in 2019[1] said that only 23 percent of line managers had been trained in people management skills.

It wasn't until ten or so years later at a different organisation, when I did stints at Cranfield and then later a year-long European leaders programme, that I learnt anything about delegation, strategy, planning, communication styles.... And even then, none of the training I received covered what I think are critical aspects of management, such as self-awareness and emotion regulation.

The training certainly didn't cover how to have the critical conversation we are going to be tackling in this book.

I am warm, relatively emotionally intelligent and a good communicator, but I made so many mistakes.

- I wanted to do a good job. I wanted people in my team to thrive. But I also wanted to be loooooved.
- I often treated people as **I** would like to be treated without an understanding of diversity of need.
- There were always certain people in my team I was more drawn to spending time with than others (causing me sometimes to be cliquey…).
- I often recruited in my own image rather than looking for people whose skills might complement mine.
- I hated conflict.
- I wasn't always clear with my team on requirements. We were all in this together, weren't we? Why should I potentially upset the apple cart by being clear and possibly ruin our relationship?
- I was (and am still) very impatient. I sometimes failed to step through a comprehensive delegation process with team members.
- When people struggled with stress – I either went into 'bending over backwards to support' overdrive, or immediately got my HR team involved because I was scared of getting it wrong.

- I am, as I discovered much later in life, plagued with perfectionist tendencies which also made it very difficult for me to take (what can be the gold dust!) feedback on board.

During my early manager years, I was appreciated by my bosses for 'getting things done' but had been promoted so quickly I lacked two foundational aspects.

Firstly, I didn't really understand the nuts and bolts of what any of my team members did.

Secondly, I had a lack of foundation as a human being.

I was still young; at only 23 I had experienced so little adversity. White, middle class, fairly academic and articulate, I had all the conditions in place for success. My parents were happy together, and my childhood, whilst I felt a bit stifled about a perceived need for conformity, was secure and happy. This should of course (and ultimately does) provide me with excellent foundations. However, it was precisely this lack of understanding of how cruel life can be, and how 'pulling your socks up' isn't always possible, which led me to being out of my depth as a human being, often in those early days.

These two foundational 'deficits' made me driven, in those early days, by the insecurity of being 'found out'. This is sometimes called imposter syndrome, but I believe, in retrospect, at 23, I was indeed something of an imposter!

I was already a hard worker, but that same imposter syndrome made me double down. It has arguably built a habit for very hard work which I still struggle to detach from to this day.

It encouraged my (undiscovered) perfectionist streak to go into overdrive. It made me, in those early days, sometimes competitive with people in my team who knew more than I did.

At 26, on my third promotion in the organisation, I took on a larger team where several of my very good friends worked. Two of my friends were not performing in their roles and one of them had chronic health issues. Having no idea how to address this, but being under no illusions that I needed to, I used the new HR support with its procedures. I can still picture myself handing them formal letters, inviting them to attend a performance meeting.

I could not look myself in the mirror for weeks afterwards. I hated myself for how I had handled it.

At 28, I was head hunted to go to a very different kind of business – one steeped already in formality and very much in the command and control mode. I was hired as a Director; a manager of managers. One morning my recently appointed sales manager came into my office and told me that his dad had taken his own life that day and that he had been the one to find him. Stunned and absolutely out of my depth, I had no idea of what to say or do – awkwardly hugging him, sending him home and then managing his return to work, way too early, two weeks later, completely ineptly.

Managers need:

- Empathy – often afforded by life experience
- Self-awareness, self-management and emotion regulation skills

- Training in the tools that enable them to get the best out of people
- A basic understanding of the legal framework in which they operate

I know I have not painted myself in the best light but, fortunately, I wasn't uniformly terrible, and I have got better as I've got older, more empathetic… and trained!

My biggest work achievement (aside from starting my own business) was that in my forties I turned a business, which was declining and losing money, into profit and growth within nine months, when two previous Directors had failed to do so. That was a great example of building vulnerable relationships with my team and a demonstration of how culture ultimately trumps strategy.

We ripped up what we had tried and started again on a regular basis. By then I had learnt a lot about how not to do things.

I had also, by the time I reached that age, been through an unhappy marriage and a move to Australia where I gave birth to my daughter in traumatic circumstances. I had then suffered from some sort of anxiety, moved back to the UK and got divorced. The divorce led to single parenthood – which I still navigate today.

I have always been self-reflective, but I firmly believe that without those difficult life experiences I would have had much less empathy. The challenges I have now experienced – getting older, dealing with life's inevitable struggles – have also helped me become less fearful, less concerned about impressing others, and to operate further and further in line with my own value system.

I still make mistakes.

But I can (mostly) look myself in the mirror each day. If not, I reflect on my mistakes and try to clean them up.

Nobody is perfect at being a boss or at having challenging conversations. We are all only human and subject to blind spots and hidden patterns.

With small steps all the time – mostly in understanding myself better – and by working with experts and coaches myself – I improve. (Slightly!)

INTRODUCTION

Kaizen

The Japanese art of continuous improvement

Was the job of people management in an organisation always this difficult?

Surely not.

In the past, prevalent command-and-control cultures meant that managers could have a pretty straightforward approach. There was little thought about inclusion and equity, remote work wasn't really a thing and there was somehow just less work to do.

The cherry on the cake over the last few years has been that stress and mental health issues (whether home- or work-related) have become a significant challenge in the workplace, and managers must have the skills and knowledge to navigate this, whilst maintaining boundaries of some sort.

This is no mean feat.

These days the challenges for line managers are greater than they have ever been.

When I share this book title with a room full of them, "I'm a boss, not a shrink" they often nod vehemently.

"Yes, **that is** how we feel!"

The problems aren't going away

This book is for the managers who have to wear all the hats as they navigate the people in their workplace. They are **not** shrinks – but there is now an expectation that they know how to have those needed and difficult conversations with people struggling in the workplace.

These may be difficulties related to work, or equally to do with something in their home life. Given that sickness absence and long-term disability due to mental health issues are currently rising exponentially, alongside an expectation that we will show care for our employees, the world has become so much more complex for managers to navigate. This book will allude to some of the reasons behind this newfound complexity. It will also guide you through:

- How to spot the signs that someone in your team is struggling – with life, with work, with their mental health.
- How to listen effectively and demonstrate care.
- What kind of support you could offer and the boundaries you could consider setting.
- What duty of care looks like for a manager.
- How we also look after ourselves effectively (no mean feat)!

This book is written particularly for managers because addressing the behaviour of managers and leaders in an organisation will make the biggest difference to your company wellbeing than any other initiative.

Managers also have duties in this area that they are usually not trained to understand.

Over the last seven years I have been honing my specialism, training managers and offering talks teaching organisations how to have good conversations about mental health. If you'd like me to talk to your organisation, my details are at the front of this book.

I work mostly with large organisations where I offer training and talks both online and face to face and have worked across construction, retail, pharma, media, energy and transport. I use actors to help demonstrate some of these principles and offer a safe space for people to watch a good (and a bad) conversation to play out.

I have observed that a manager's concerns in opening these conversations are the same everywhere. Whilst internationally, some cultures may find a direct approach to asking if someone is OK a lot easier than others, most people worry about getting it wrong and making the situation worse.

We also find that running training like this in organisations can not only benefit participants' working lives, but often they share that they had much better conversations with their partner or children as a result of trying some of these methodologies.

Poor wellbeing is unsafe

It is becoming more and more apparent that good wellbeing is of utmost importance to the running of a business – in fact they are integrally linked – what can be overlooked is how much wellbeing is also layered into safety. Whilst I have been a manager of large and small teams, my background is in health and safety – where the hidden hazard of poor wellbeing has been largely under explored. This is partly, I believe, because only some incident and accident investigation processes even consider wellbeing and human factors – which is actually mind boggling to me.

It is, however, accepted that fatigue is a major contributory factor to accidents and major disasters in the workplace, but what does the data show about whether mental illness and mental distress are also causal factors?

In 2006, the Keil Centre examined the link between psychological ill health, anxiety, depression and safety, and concluded, (as we all intuitively know) that all of these factors can interfere with an individual's performance[2].

It is no surprise that the impact of mental distress, stress, depression, anxiety, or other mental illness will have an impact on an individual's level of cognition and attention.

A study of the airline industry in 2018 found that pilot mental disorders were implicated in 17 accidents and incidents over the previous 35 years, including nine fatal accidents that resulted in 576 deaths according to another source. The study identified several risk factors for pilot mental disorders, such as negative life events, substance abuse, personality traits, and occupational stressors. The study also highlighted the challenges of detecting and treating pilot mental disorders in the aviation context[3].

Health and safety professionals have already accepted and attempt to mitigate the impact of fatigue, drugs and alcohol, violence and harassment at work. Is it too big a stretch to start to consider burnout, bullying managers, a culture of 'performance at all costs', lack of perceived justice, micro-management, poor pay and conditions, and worry about finances (just as some examples)?

International applicability

Healthy Work Company is based in the United Kingdom and yet we train this programme internationally. It is worth noting that, whatever your nationality, if you notice someone struggling, then listening and signposting skills are useful as a manager. However, there are a few trip hazards of which we urge you to be aware.

Firstly, legal frameworks around the world are subtly different; for example, countries vary in the amount of formal support they insist on in law. In many EU countries, for example, there is a requirement for a company doctor to make recommendations on reasonable adjustments, which may place less of an onus on the team manager.

The requirement to do an organisational stress or psychosocial risk assessment often sits in a country's health and safety law (enforcement is patchy but growing) and there is an equivalent of the UK Equality Act which protects the right to fair treatment for those with an ongoing mental health issue (under disability discrimination).

Some countries have additionally legislated for the reporting of workplace-related suicide; France famously has very tight laws relating to working time; Spain entered menopause leave into the statute book in February 2023. Australia has recently tightened its approach to psychosocial risk assessment in workplaces, with the state of New South Wales making it explicit within law that this is a requirement for organisations.

Some countries have heavy union involvement in mental health and related policies and, in others, insurance is a driver of activity in the arena of stress management.

Secondly, we would be foolish to ignore cultural context, particularly different attitudes to mental health, with a higher degree of shame and stigma in some cultures than others. For example, in some Middle Eastern countries, suicide is considered a crime under Sharia law (based on Islamic principles). This can create a barrier for people who need help or support for their mental health, as they may fear legal consequences or social stigma[4].

And let's not ignore different cultural communication methods. I highly recommend Erin Meyer's *The Culture Map*. This book presents research on high- and low-context cultures – that is, how precise, simple and clear communication is lauded in certain countries, where others expect you to read between the lines. It looks at direct and indirect communication preferences and, finally, the importance placed on business relationships, loyalty and trust which means that in certain countries in the world the personal is highly relevant to business and in others work relationships are considerably more superficial.

In essence, if you manage a global team then read Erin's book. What this book does is present some principles of best practice as well as some considerations which I believe are mostly globally applicable.

I hope that, in reading this book, you will be encouraged to start those conversations with people in your team who are struggling, to hold yourself back from the panicky feeling that you need to solve their problems for them and also to continually work on your self-awareness. As managers we unconsciously create the way people relate to us – and continuing to dig into what makes us tick as individuals, and why this will have an impact on those around us, is critical.

PART 1:
THE PERFECT STORM

CHAPTER 1:

HOW ARE YOU REALLY?

It's business, leave your personal life at the door.
Anon

When I was growing up there was a strict divide between work and home.

My dad put his briefcase down at the end of the day and didn't think about work until his commute the following morning. There was no question of working at weekends and he would have been mystified at the idea of checking in to the office on his holidays. Jobs were often for life – he lasted 30 years at the same place – with a final salary pension at the end.

My mum was already unusual in being a housewife – other mums had gone back to work – but this made life at our house pretty quiet and relaxed. She was responsible for the house and us children; my dad (who brought home the proverbial bacon) had his dinner on the table for 7pm.

That divide between home and work went mostly the other way of course. We may have enquired, in our mostly male-led workplaces, about our colleagues' personal lives and shown an interest in holidays and children, but we held onto the idea that we should leave the difficulties of our personal lives at the door when it came to work.

A far cry from the 'bring your whole self to work' mantra of many modern corporations.

And yes, workloads were more manageable, people stayed married – happily or unhappily – lives were arguably narrower with fewer choices, and less steeped in individual overt drama than the era of huge social change we now navigate.

The world has changed unthinkably in the last 50 years.

These changes are reflected in the world of work.

Speed of response is now furious, enabled by technology which pings at us demanding we swing into action. With rapidly shifting priorities, there is an expectation that we will work out of hours or until the job is done. This is known as 'work intensification' and whether you are a cleaner, a nurse, a teacher, a site manager, an event organiser, the head of a bank – whatever your role – it is the scourge of the modern workplace.

Low control is also a feature of many modern workplaces, with productivity in certain jobs so systematised that there is no room for individuals to discuss the how, when and the where (even toilet breaks may be monitored). In the UK in 1992, 71 percent of employees reported having 'a great deal' of control over how hard they worked; by 2017 this share had fallen to 46 percent[5].

Depending on where you are in the world, corporate structures are usually less hierarchical than they were, and you can't always 'tell' people what to do. Influence has to be earned through networking with our peers – if I don't know you, I am less likely to help you – all of which takes additional time and energy.

Workplaces are no longer organised around straight, white, able-bodied males: equality, equity, diversity and inclusion have become a key part of creating a sustainable workforce – adding both complexity to management and reward to those organisations that can harness them.

Our jobs are more precarious, yet many of us expect more from them than we used to – not just financial reward but also growth and learning, human connection, sometimes even meaning and purpose. Good work **is** good for us.

Our personal lives have also become more complex. Women are now navigating corporate careers, often at the same time as managing the load (or at least the cognitive load!) for homes, children and/or elderly parents. A huge rise in divorce has made this even more fragile. Working single parents (of which I am one) make up 25 percent of the population in the UK – with 90 percent of those females[6].

Those home admin matters that my mum took all day to do are now completed in the free seconds and minutes of the day.

The art of rest has been largely lost – unless it consists of snoring in front of Netflix at nine o'clock, determined not to go to bed as 'I haven't had an evening'.

Even prior to COVID, we were training workforces who were run ragged.

People who felt that between work, the commute, the running of a house, children, elderly parents and a social life, that as much as they often really enjoyed their challenging work (or the people they worked with), they were stuck. Stuck because of mortgages and pension arrangements and societal expectation – and stuck between the balance of their often-true enjoyment of the pressure and learning afforded by their work and the knowledge that in reality, with their work and home life, it was all too much.

And then came COVID and global lockdowns.

All of a sudden there was a new perspective as some of us could work from home.

Whilst this could be challenging when it might be in a kitchen or bedroom, and consist partly of home schooling, many also found they liked spending more time with their families and putting the washing on in the working day. Perhaps not all the time, but a lot of it.

Post COVID, hybrid-working arrangements have also created increasing management challenges.

There is now a clear two-tier system with those who can work from anywhere, and those who work in a job where you have to be physically present on site – in a warehouse, in a shop or factory – in order to do the work. There are greater management challenges in having those difficult conversations remotely and greater cultural challenges in creating some semblance of workplace culture over very different workforces, many of whom will rarely meet.

For those who were fortunate to gain some flexibility, COVID made us re-evaluate priorities. What does success look like to me? Does it really all revolve around my job?

COVID and lockdowns also led, according to the World Health Organisation, to a 25 percent global increase of stress, anxiety and depression by February 2022[7].

The mental health impact of being locked down and the uncertainty brought about by COVID caused many businesses to ensure that teams held informal video get-togethers. There were more manager check-ins and a culture of greater vulnerability was encouraged, in which we told each other how we really were – rather than saying the standard, "I'm fine. How are you?"

Where we had already seen an increasing trend towards openness at work, it suddenly got messy.

As we now navigate hybrid working, a cost-of-living crisis and are in the midst of negotiating a new social contract with polarised views on right and wrong, it hasn't got any easier. And we are all tired.

In the meantime, managers and employees are struggling on.

Not only are managers spotting signs of someone in their teams every now and then who may need further support with stress or health issues, but they are having these conversations every day.

Often those manager conversations are held with no training, with no knowledge of the legal framework, and with all the discomfort and fear of saying the wrong thing.

As managers, we are normal human beings. Normal human beings who often see our role in a conversation such as these as advice-givers or problem-solvers, or providing the benefit of our own experience.

The taking on of other's problems as well as our own.

The being eaten up with guilt and shame when we get it wrong,

And the lack of knowledge of our duties as a manager or of what options there are to support an individual.

Alongside the managers, we also find very stretched HR teams called upon to hand-hold from the beginning to the end of the process. They might have more expertise than the manager, but they are often still groping for answers themselves.

Summary

- The world of work is impacted by changes outside of our working lives.
- Poor wellbeing is an increasing risk in our workplaces and yet managers are often not trained to have these difficult conversations.

CHAPTER 2:

THE UNFORESEEN CONSEQUENCES OF PROGRESS

Life can only be understood backwards; but it must be lived forwards.
Kierkegaard

We are still animals

At the time of writing, in July 2023, the use of SSRIs (anti-depressants also used to combat anxiety) had risen to 12.8 percent of the population in the UK. In the USA, that usage is 13.2 percent[8].

Just take a moment to absorb that.

This means one in eight people has a clinically diagnosed anxiety disorder or depression.

This shocking statistic may partially be a testament to the lack of available therapists in the NHS to conduct talking therapies. Some research also bears out that, now that we are happier to talk about it, the incidence of diagnosis of mental illness is greater than in the past. Most of us, however, would also agree in recent times the workplace has become more full on and challenging, alongside the new issues presented by COVID, but even prior to the pandemic huge societal changes were having an impact on our mental health.

Life has changed immeasurably over the last 50 to 100 years. So much could be seen as better for human beings (though the news would make us think it is all so much worse). Women are much freer – with ability to control their own finances, for example; society is more accepting of diversity; we are generally wealthier (though unequal wealth distribution is another issue…); technology makes what was slow and hard in the past, quick and easy.

However, as always, progress has unintended consequences, and our brains and bodies, arguably, did not evolve to deal with the way we live today.

When animals are kept in captivity (not the way they are 'supposed' to live), they may develop a range of abnormal behaviours such as pacing, repetitive movements, self-mutilation and aggression. These behaviours are thought to be caused by the stress and boredom of captivity, as well as the lack of space, stimulation, and social interaction that wild animals would normally have in their natural habitat. This is known as 'zoochosis' or 'zoo animal behaviour syndrome'.

Is there a correlation here with human beings?

Our ancestors were hunter gatherers, physically active with outdoor lives, who had to survive potential threats everywhere. Even if you don't do a desk job, do you think brains and bodies were built for the way we live today?

Our brains were built for survival, but our stress response system is triggered by events that have nothing to do with life or death – usually these days about an uncertainty in the future – which we simply can't resolve.

The negativity bias – the fact that we may catastrophise – is our helpful brain noticing threat, which served us in a survival environment.

Our clever brains also build habits, with a little dopamine reward, so we don't have to use executive brain power to get through the day. These habits might include some immediately pleasing, but long-term fairly unhealthy ones such as:

1. Binge-watching TV shows or movies
2. Overeating or eating unhealthy takeaways
3. Too much drinking, smoking or drug use
4. Gambling or playing video games excessively
5. Social media scrolling, arguing with strangers from behind a keyboard, or seeking validation from likes and comments
6. Answering every call, every text and every email the minute it comes in
7. Compulsive shopping or online shopping
8. Working excessively 'until it is all done' (It is never done)

Anyone fancy shouting "Bingo?"

The modern world is characterised by constant stimulation and distraction, which can be overwhelming for our brains. Our attention is constantly pulled in different directions by notifications, emails and social media, making it difficult to focus on important tasks or engage in deep, reflective thinking.

Our modern lifestyle frequently involves a great deal of sedentary behaviour, a high-calorie diet and exposure to environmental toxins, which can have negative effects on our physical and mental health. These factors can contribute to a range of health problems, including obesity, diabetes and depression.

The way our individual brains work is simply not conducive to the modern world.

COVID changed us

And then came a global pandemic.

Even if we managed to avoid the trauma of being infected, hospitalised or losing loved ones to the disease, the consequences for all of us were enormous, from social and economic, to disruption and uncertainty, to isolation and loneliness.

During COVID we saw a 25 percent increase in depression and anxiety according to the World Health Organisation[9], and many demographics continue to be disproportionately impacted. This includes children and young people who experienced disrupted education and social development.

Changes in society and social mores

Many people, having been forced to step off the hamster wheel of their routines during COVID, did revaluate some aspects of their lives. One of those was the renewed understanding of the importance of human connection. Some of us reconnected with our families or got more involved in our local communities; others re-evaluated relationships and decided whom we wanted to spend more time with.

Our evolutionary history as a species shows that our ancestors lived in small groups or tribes, which provided them with social support, protection and a means of sharing resources.

Living in tribes allowed humans to work together to hunt, gather food, build shelters and protect themselves from predators. Humans needed this cooperation and developed a strong tendency to form social bonds.

This physical connection has been increasingly lost as we move away from our families for education or work (or because we can!) and we are often too busy to create a local community. Our 'close relationships' are often played out online instead.

Long prior to the pandemic, Johann Hari pointed out in his book *Lost Connections*[10] that humans are social animals who need meaningful connections with others to thrive, and that the breakdown of these social bonds in modern society has contributed to widespread feelings of loneliness, isolation and despair.

So, whilst social media provides an easy form of daily connection with others, when the proverbial shit hits the fan, in spite of thousands of virtual connections, we can find ourselves with no one to loan us money, help us move to a new house or be a physical shoulder to cry on. A study from UK-based counselling service Relate in 2019 showed that 14 percent of people living in the UK didn't have any close friends[11]. The figure is worse for men where it is one in five. Yet, research shows us that those people around the world who live longer, happier lives often still live in communities[12].

Interestingly, the definition of 'tribe' was of course widened some time ago to encompass our country, our religion and increasingly in modern society it may be defined by our values. We hear, "Ah I have found my tribe" when we meet people who reflect our own way of viewing the world.

The pace of change of societal values is another factor that contributes to the disruptive nature of the time we are living through. This is influenced by many factors, including the decline of Christianity in many parts of the world which, whatever you think of religion, provided some pretty 'fixed' rules for living and some clear views of what was believed to be right and wrong. There have been huge changes in technology, globalisation and demographic shifts. This rapid shift in often diametrically opposing values, causes tension as people adapt to new ways of thinking and interacting with each other.

Two examples of this are that, in recent years, there has been a significant change in attitudes towards issues such as gender and sexuality, as people have become more accepting of non-traditional gender identities and sexual orientations.

Secondly, the role of men and women has been changing from traditional conventions, which existed for hundreds of years, where women were essentially the property of men. Whilst this is no longer true, we have unconsciously inherited systems and ways of being which we are now uncovering and challenging. Both this and the growth of non-traditional gender identities presents such problems in certain societies as, "What is a man; what is a woman?"

When looking deeper at inherited systems, for a chance to have the scales pulled from your eyes in terms of how many aspects of the modern world are based on data that ignores or excludes women, and how this has serious consequences for women's health, safety, education, work and more, I always recommend reading *Invisible Women* by Caroline Criado Perez[13].

We also know that women still maintain much of the cognitive load of managing children, a house, elderly parents, a social life, as well as often holding demanding jobs[14]. This certainly contributes to a rise in divorce.

But how do men navigate this new world? Let's just look at fatherhood for instance. We find systemic inequalities for men too.

Chris Stein, Advocate

Chris Stein, Director of Advocacy at Future Men (futuremen.org) and Interim CEO of Fathers' Development Foundation (www.fathersdevelopment.com) writes:

"For many men, there is an expectation – probably met with a desire – to do more in child raising, management of the home, while also maintaining social status in terms of income and career progression. While these expectations mirror those of modern motherhood, there are many areas where policy does not provide the structure for modern fatherhood. Statutory paternity leave in the UK lags far behind EU and OECD countries where the fixed leave for fathers is 8.5 and 10.4 weeks on average across those countries, as opposed to 2 weeks. Paternity is not a recognised characteristic in the Equalities Act of 2010. There are other areas, but I won't go on. Let it be said that asking a person to fulfill a role where the structure is not there for them to perform the role, is the definition of inequity."

Frustration, anger and resentment builds – none of which is good for mental health and which can lead to radicalisation. Look at the rise of popularity of Andrew Tate among young men.

Overall, the pace of change of values is a significant factor in the disruptive nature of the current age, as people adapt to new ways of thinking and interacting with each other.

My niece, Miss Maria: Intergenerational tensions

I often have very lively discussions with my highly intelligent niece, Maria, and I am reminded during these conversations that Generation Z is the most highly educated in history. I tend to get very passionate in these conversations and wonder why I feel so strongly about an issue. I reflect afterwards that whilst both she and I may think we are open-minded, we each view the world through the paradigm of our own experience, upbringing, and those we spend time with. We both think that our arguments are rational – in fact our reactions to a topic come from our habitual emotional response which we then post rationalise[15].

In the workplace you are likely to find huge generational differences in ideas around work. Older generations are more likely to embrace the status quo in terms of hard work and not prioritise work/life balance where Generation Z will prioritise flexible working and will look for workplaces where inclusion is genuine. Younger workers may be happier to talk about their mental health issues and may use different coping mechanisms for mental distress, such as self-harm.

My niece, by the way, is an extraordinary human being (as is my nephew!) but one of the things I love about her is that even though we argue very strongly with each other, this does not mean we value or love each other less. This is remarkable because it is rare. In the UK, in these times, the culture wars dictate that our beliefs are seen to define us as good or bad humans.

Individualism and wealth

Our increasing individualism may lead us to high expectations of life and a tendency to tie our value and our success as a human to feeling happy. But research shows that expectations can be the enemy of happiness[16] and that every human being goes through difficulties in life when it would be crazy to expect them to be happy (not in the hedonic sense). It is normal to feel grief and pain, there can be lessons for us in difficult emotions, but today we struggle with those when we see them in ourselves and others. We think 'there's something wrong'.

Furthermore, in recent decades, whilst there is undoubtedly much greater wealth around, it is going to an increasingly small number of people. In my lifetime, the middle classes have grown, and we all gained from economic progress. But recently, our systems have started to lead to an enormous and increasing gap between rich and poor in many countries around the world. For those living in poverty, financial insecurity and lack of access to basic necessities like healthcare, housing, and food can cause a great deal of stress and anxiety.

The impact of inequality is, surprisingly, not only felt by those in poverty. Studies have found that people who live in more unequal societies tend to report lower levels of happiness and wellbeing, even if they themselves are not poor. This effect is thought to occur because income inequality can lead to social comparisons and feelings of relative deprivation, where people compare their own situation to others who are better off and feel dissatisfied as a result.

Healthcare systems, such as our own National Health Service in the UK, are ailing – particularly (but not uniquely) when it comes to funding for mental health services. As a consequence, when we do become ill, it is increasingly difficult to access treatment.

Good mental health and wellbeing of citizens and the sustainability of our planet don't yet seem to be the primary concerns of our governments. Tackling these issues would mean significant changes in policies and societal attitudes.

Meanwhile our 24-hour, advertising-led media models are optimised to produce conflict and stress. 'If it bleeds it leads' and social media platforms lead to echo chambers and fake news.

A perfect storm has now coalesced above us which has created these mental health issues we are now so familiar with. Combined with increased workloads and frenetic pace of work, it is no wonder so many of us are struggling.

It is easy to get panicked or despondent.

I am optimistic and believe we will claw our way out of this chaotic stage for human beings. However, for now, how do we make things better for ourselves?

Individually, we need to come off autopilot, look at what is important to us and which of our habits (work and personal) support our overall wellbeing and happiness. We need to look at what is in our control.

We need to learn to listen to each other better, to stop judging each other because we hold a different opinion but try to understand what lies behind that opinion.

Societally we need to work to produce better systems which contribute to happiness, wellbeing and sustainability.

Summary

- Our brains were optimised for survival, and modern life frequently triggers our stress response system. Usually, it isn't a matter of life and death when it is triggered.
- Modern society is not conducive to good mental health. Technology, changes in social mores, and financial inequality are contributing to the mental health crisis we see today.
- Whilst as a species we are benefiting from progress, we need also to consider how we deal with its unintended consequences.

CHAPTER 3:

WELLBEING AT WORK

If I am walking along a river and I see someone drowning, my first impulse is to jump in and save them. But then I notice more people in the river, and I see that I can't possibly save them all by myself. So I start to walk upstream to find out why so many people are falling into the river in the first place, and to see if there's anything I can do to prevent it.
William Wilberforce

The business case is urgent

Only ten years ago, wellbeing was a minor consideration in a company's strategy and was generally owned by HR benefits teams. It was made up of such things as fruit Fridays, yoga, and cycle-to-work schemes to make people feel warm and fuzzy about the workplace and to support their physical health.

Over the last six or seven years, we started to consider the mental as well as physical health of our employees and during COVID, as we watched people suffering, the new workplace discipline of 'wellbeing' quickly became a corporate priority.

Wellbeing at work
2016-2023

Physical health

Mental illness destigmatisation

Business focused wellbeing

Cycle to work/Yoga /Fruit

Mental Health First Aid

Covid specific intervention- managing stress/Wellbeing days

Manager training/Senior Management Team training

ISO 45003 Wellbeing risk assessment/ Sustainable cultural approach

Basic mental health awareness training is a key tenet of most wellbeing strategies. But increasingly, with mental health services (psychologists, psychiatrists and counsellors) across the globe underfunded and stretched, big business is picking up the slack. Large employers are offering Employee Assistance Programmes (EAPs), providing counselling, financial and legal advice, as well as online doctor support, fertility advice, neurodiversity assessments, fitness and nutrition advice, financial wellbeing and even private medical care.

Small businesses, meanwhile, are often stuck with overstretched doctor services.

Wellbeing is now a, if not **the**, key risk for businesses and of critical importance to people sustainability. With soaring long-term sickness/disability due to mental ill health, a lack of available staff, low engagement and increasingly stressed employees, Gallup's global survey at the end of 2022[17] says that employees are feeling even more stressed than they did in 2020 (the previous all-time high). Meanwhile:

- The UK risks a shrinking workforce caused by long-term sickness, as there has been a sharp increase in 'economic inactivity' – working-age adults who are not in work or looking for jobs – from 21.6 percent in 2019 to 23.4 percent in 2020.[18]

- The number of people out of work due to long-term sickness in the UK rose by half a million, from 2 million in 2019 to 2.5 million in 2020.[19]

This new discipline of 'wellbeing' is paved with good intentions, but often ill-defined, unmeasured and either placed at too junior a level to make a significant cultural difference, or between HR and Health & Safety – without clarity on who is responsible for what.

As we can see above, most initiatives focus on individual wellbeing – whether supporting mental or physical health – encouraging people to understand and look after themselves better or picking them up when they fall. However, good wellbeing, as we have already seen in this book, is very much related to the world or system we inhabit.

This interplay between the environment – the community – and the individual is appreciated to a far greater extent in Asian cultures. Many Western cultures place a far greater burden on individual rights and responsibilities.

But ask yourself this – is it easier to be well:

- in a society or community which looks after you when you are sick, unemployed or homeless?
- in an organisation where you are paid fairly, you feel you do good work, you have a good manager and know that the organisation will look after you if you are sick?
- in a team where your boss checks in regularly to see if you are happy, if you have the right resources, if your workload is right for you?

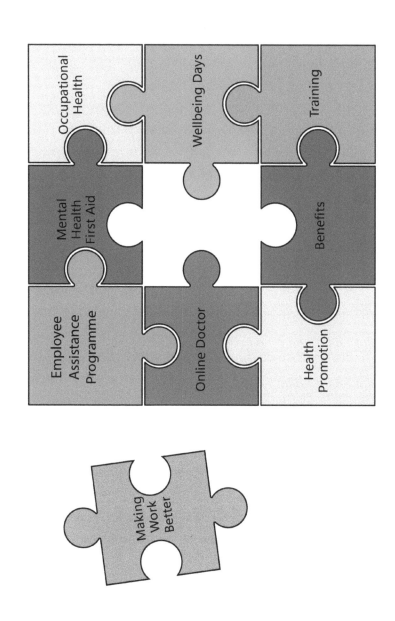

Creating a culture of wellbeing is about creating conditions in your workplace in which your teams can thrive.

If as businesses we focus on training in resilience and supporting individuals with counselling when things go wrong, we are missing a critical part of the puzzle.

The argument is clear. Whoever takes responsibility for the coordination and expert recommendations for your wellbeing programme, the strategy needs to be understood and ultimately owned by the Board because it needs to be integral to your overall mission and values. It intertwines with Health and Safety, People and Culture, EDI (Equality, Diversity and Inclusion) and now with ESG (Environmental Social and Governance).

In 2021, Healthy Work Company ran a survey which showed that whilst 92 percent of our contacts had a wellbeing 'strategy', only 29 percent had trained their senior team[20].

Because the ownership of wellbeing often sits too far down the business hierarchy, it is not hard to understand why the systemic, cultural issues often go into the 'too hard' box.

It stands to reason that decisions senior managers make, their own role modelling and the quality of people management in your organisation are actually the most critical places to start. If you truly want to make a difference to wellbeing where you work, as well as mental health awareness and interventions to support people when they are sick, focus on:

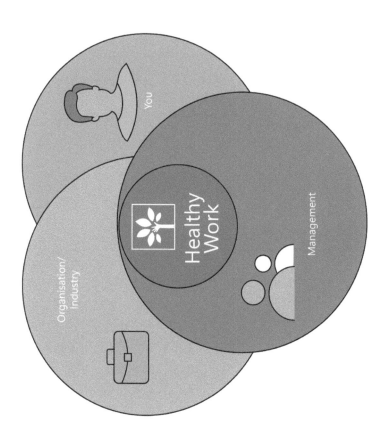

Healthy Work

You

Organisation/Industry

Management

- Understanding what causes stress in your workplace. Define the problems really clearly so that you can measure them, draw them to the attention of your senior team and problem-solve with them.
- Selecting and providing ongoing training to directors, senior managers and managers with both performance **and** care in mind. And hope they are self-aware!

The causes of stress in your workplace

Is doing an organisational stress risk assessment a requirement for your workplace in your country?

I bet you didn't know that it was in the UK!

Within the Health and Safety at Work etc Act 1974, and in many countries around the world, stress is treated as a health and safety risk to be assessed, designed out or mitigated.

Employers have a duty to provide a safe system of work, including providing any necessary training, information and equipment to ensure the safety and health of employees. This duty extends to the prevention of harm to employees' mental health due to work-related stress.

The Management Standards from the Health and Safety Executive (HSE)[21] is a risk assessment tool that includes six areas of work design that, if not properly managed, are associated with poor mental health and wellbeing and can lead to work-related stress. These six areas are:

1. Demands
2. Control
3. Support
4. Relationships
5. Role
6. Change

However, in the UK at least, many health and safety professionals themselves are not aware of this and will instead focus on **individual** stress risk assessments – which are put in place when someone, for example, is returning to work following sickness absence for work-related stress.

This lack of knowledge shouldn't really be excused now because there has been so much education available around the issue in the last few years, but lack of enforcement from the HSE means that many organisations turn a blind eye to this requirement.

The arrival of the new international wellbeing standard ISO45003,[22] which is a companion standard to the health and safety one ISO45001, expands on these six factors from HSE and ironically, because it looks at a significantly greater number of factors, is more holistic and more helpful. It includes factors such as engagement, leadership, fair treatment, pay, discrimination, and actually breaks those out into a much larger number of questions.

In many organisations, the lack of a joint approach between HR and health & safety means that they miss the fact that the pulse surveys, engagement surveys already being run by HR teams, will hold a lot of the key stress risk factors already, but they have not been brought together into a formal health and safety risk assessment.

The wonderful thing about a stress or psychosocial risk assessment is that it can provide some real areas of focus for your wellbeing strategy. It should be done team by team or function by function dependent on the size of your organisation. Even if done organisationally initially, it can highlight those areas that you already know you really need to tackle but ensures you tackle them in a prioritised manner – trying to design them out first and foremost.

In many organisations these risks are related to work demands, low control and poor management.

Other inputs to your stress or psychosocial risk assessment might be from:

- Employee forums and engagement sessions
- Team stress risk assessments (see below)
- Performance appraisals and 360-degree feedback
- Anonymous input from mental health first aid conversations, Employee Assistance Programme (EAP), occupational health
- Grievance processes and exit interviews

Senior management must be involved in discussing the findings because they are far better placed to address the pace of work, the type of work, resources and management/leadership culture.

As a team manager, even if your senior team is not ready to do an organisational stress risk assessment, there is nothing to stop you as a manager asking pertinent questions of your team which will enable you to identify and prevent stress before it causes someone to struggle. You can ask them:

"What do you love about working here?"

"What do you hate and what really stresses you out about working here?"

You might find that many of the answers are organisational factors that are out of your control (so feed them in!) but look at what **is** in your influence and within your control. For example, are there agreements you can come to about communication, working hours and what constitutes an emergency?

Summary

- Over the last ten years there have been many changes in the way we have managed wellbeing, and the current climate has made it a key business risk.
- Organisations are generally tackling wellbeing using interventions such as mental health awareness training and supportive services for when employees get sick, such as Employee Assistance programmes.
- Very few organisations have tackled the cultural, systemic issues that are integral to a wellbeing strategy and which are key to creating an environment in which people can thrive at work.
- Your senior team has to be involved in creating a wellbeing strategy as it is integral to the organisation's mission and values.
- A stress or psychosocial risk assessment for the organisation will help identify the causes of stress, but as a manager you can do this with your team.

PART 2: UNDERSTANDING MENTAL HEALTH, WELLBEING AND STRESS

CHAPTER 4:

WHAT DO WE MEAN BY MENTAL HEALTH AND WELLBEING?

We start from the position that the correct way to view mental health is that we all have it and we fluctuate between thriving, struggling and being ill and possibly off work.
Farmer-Stevenson Report on Thriving at Work, 2017[23]

t's worth saying that the term mental health has become somewhat tarnished. People hear it and think of mental illness. In fact, many of the very early training interventions in this space were indeed mostly about explaining and destigmatising mental illnesses.

In my business, we have tended to focus on discussing 'mental distress' because whilst diagnosed mental illness is becoming a real problem for individuals and businesses – particularly anxiety and depression – even without meeting the criteria for diagnosis, life in these uncertain and chaotic times can be incredibly stressful. We may not be mentally ill, but we are often struggling.

Wellbeing is a less-tarnished term but subject to numerous definitions. Two conceptual approaches dominate the research on wellbeing:

- The objective approach examines the objective components of a good life.
- The subjective approach examines people's subjective evaluations of their lives.

I always prefer to talk about wellbeing rather than mental health because mental and physical health are inexorably intertwined. We have somehow separated physical and mental health as if they were two very different things. This Cartesian idea of dualism is very embedded in our society and underpins the artificial conceptual separation of 'physical' and 'mental' disorders in western medical practice.

In organisations we do need to understand our sickness absence data – we may divide it into work- or non-work-related stress, musculoskeletal disorders, gastric problems, colds and flu – which of course has merit. But so much of this is intertwined. Our physical ill health for example, is often underpinned by stress. It is also rarely possible to say with absolute certainty that what has caused someone to go off with stress is entirely related to their work or their personal life. Often the problems occur together.

Rashes or stress?

In my last corporate role, I worked with a fantastic, hard-working man 'P' who showed such diligence and was such an ideal team member that I gave him a bigger job. In the first few weeks of having that role, he answered yes to everything I asked of him and was a well-loved member of the team.

One day he came in and I noticed he had rashes all up his arms. We went to a meeting room, and I asked if he was using a different washing powder or had been to the doctor. "No," he said, "I have no idea what it is about." "You don't think you are stressed, do you?" I said.

He burst into tears.

With two very young children at home, his wife had recently returned to work and they had no family support within reach. I had also promoted him, and a combination of my style (probably a bit intimidating) and his desire to please had not enabled him to explain where he needed support in the role, so he felt that he was overstretched and failing there too.

We agreed that he would go straight home via the doctor. The doctor signed him off for two weeks during which he looked at how his family situation could work better. On his return to work we decided a reasonable adjustment would be for him to return to his old work with review after a period.

A continuum of mental health

In 2017, Theresa May commissioned a report on the mental health of UK workplaces and the quote at the beginning of this chapter comes from that report. This idea that we all have mental health and that it fluctuates is from the work of Professor Corey Keyes and his model 'The continuum of flourishing'. We might aim to be flourishing or thriving – which suggests we are happy and have hope for the future. When a few things go out of balance we might have moderate mental health. If this gets worse – perhaps we are overthinking all the time, can't sleep, feel anxious or low in a way which starts to interfere with our daily life – we might be languishing or struggling.

Once we are given a diagnosis of a mental illness, it can be a lengthy process to recover and flourish again or to find our way to flourishing **with** a mental illness, as people such as Stephen Fry and Alastair Campbell do. My daughter, Rosie, who had a diagnosis of obsessive-compulsive disorder in 2021 has taken two years to get to a place of moderate mental health and mental illness.

Any one of us can develop mental illness. In the field of epigenetics, it is suggested that genes can be triggered by circumstances. Stressful life events (including work or unemployment), difficult childhoods, poverty, discrimination, poor physical health – all of these can feed into the development of a diagnosed mental illness.

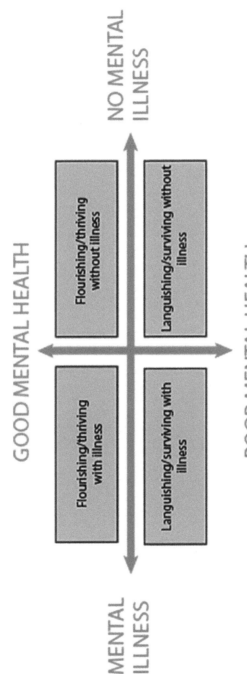

MENTAL ILLNESS

GOOD MENTAL HEALTH

NO MENTAL ILLNESS

Flourishing/thriving with illness

Flourishing/thriving without illness

Languishing/surviving with illness

Languishing/surviving without illness

POOR MENTAL HEALTH

I know mental illness exists. I have seen it first hand in my own family. But it is also normal to go through difficult life events, unwelcome negative emotions and to overthink sometimes – and this doesn't necessarily mean we are ill.

When life gets really, really hard, are we ill?

At the end of 2020, during COVID, my dear mum died of a heart attack suddenly, aged 77. She left us (even though we had told her so many times not to do this!) with my dad who had dementia which quickly became quite severe Alzheimer's once she had gone. My sister and I struggled with his care – he was sectioned in hospital under the Mental Health Act at one point – and after seven months had gone by in 2021, he was put into a home near me so I visited him three or four times a week.

In February of 2021, my lovely neighbour, my second mum, also died; my daughter, was diagnosed with severe obsessive-compulsive disorder and I just couldn't seem to get help for my menopausal symptoms. At the same time, I was trying to run a business.

I tried my very best to cope and found that I couldn't. I embarked on a short-lived and ill-advised relationship with someone I hoped would 'rescue me' (an absolute fantasy) and ran away to France or Portugal regularly, leaving my ex-husband in charge of the child, the dog and the house.

My beloved dad died at the end of 2021, exactly a year after my mum.

I had a lot of support from friends, colleagues and family but I also had suggestions that I should visit the doctor to get something to 'help me through'. A shaman or psychic or therapist might have helped (and indeed I did have regular therapy and had some crazy shamanistic treatment at a retreat!) but I was struggling with grief, with life, with a temporarily horrible situation. I didn't want or need pills and I wasn't ill. Just sad.

But whilst I had been brought up to put a brave face on everything, on this occasion, I allowed myself to fall apart and to see what emerged when I put myself back together. For other people, this can be very uncomfortable to see. They don't want their friend or loved one struggling. They want you back to the happy positive version they love. (We're not always mentally ill when we fall apart.)

Gender differences in mental health

Men and women show that they are struggling with mental ill health in different ways, and how they deal with these struggles when they arise is also different. There are also generational factors to consider. Younger men may be more comfortable in talking about 'anxiety' for example, where older men may talk about 'worry'. Whilst there has been some decrease in stigma, if your workforce is predominantly male, you will need to ensure that you create an environment where it is OK to talk about struggles. Talking heads, videos or senior managers talking about their own vulnerabilities can really help here.

- Women may be more likely to experience symptoms of anxiety and depression, such as feeling overwhelmed, having difficulty sleeping, and physical symptoms such as headaches or stomach problems. Men, on the other hand, may be more likely to experience symptoms of anger or irritability, loss of libido, and may be less likely to talk about feelings of sadness or hopelessness.

- Women may be more likely to seek social support and talk about their feelings, whereas men may be more likely to engage in behaviours that distract them from their problems, such as working long hours or engaging in risky behaviours, drugs or alcohol abuse.

- Women may be more likely to seek help for mental health concerns, such as seeing a therapist or talking to their doctor, whereas men may be more reluctant to seek help or may delay seeking help until symptoms have become severe.

- Men may be more likely to experience stigma around mental health concerns, and may be less likely to seek help due to fears of being seen as weak or vulnerable.

When discussing gender differences in mental health, it's important to recognise that the experiences of transgender people may differ from those of cisgender individuals. Transgender people face unique challenges related to their gender identity, including discrimination, stigma, and lack of access to healthcare.

Research shows that transgender individuals have higher rates of depression, anxiety, and other mental health conditions compared to the general population.

Step in before they break

The trick for managers and for those who care about their workforce is to support them **before** they develop mental illness, because the route back to flourishing can be long and rocky. Tertiary support is hard to find, stigma still exists, and finding the requisite energy to pursue recovery when there is no set route can make this a long winding road.

A manager's job is to:

- notice when pressure becomes stress.
- take a preventative approach by asking questions.
- create an environment in which people can tell you the truth. (This is called creating psychological safety.)

Let's normalise pointing out our concerns early – before pressure becomes stress. Ask with genuine interest whether someone is OK. Say what our worries are and what we have noticed about our co-worker's current behaviour.

Summary

- We all have mental health and it fluctuates throughout our lives.
- Struggling with our mental health is normal from time to time.
- As managers, if we can support people before they become too stressed to function, or develop a mental illness, we can potentially avoid lengthy sickness absences.

CHAPTER 5:

WHEN PRESSURE BECOMES STRESS

Too much work and too much energy kill a man just as
effectively as too much-assorted vice or too much drink.
Rudyard Kipling

If you ask a group of people whether stress is good for you, the majority will say… "Hmm, a little bit".

The famous Yerkes-Dodson stress curve[24] shows that there's an optimal level of pressure that helps you to perform at your best. Too little and you're not motivated enough, but too much and you become overwhelmed, and your performance suffers. It's all about finding that sweet spot where you're motivated and focused, but not so stressed out that you can't think straight.

Technically, stress is the body's response to pressure or challenge. And some pressure and challenge are good for us. How we react to those differs from individual to individual, and indeed from day to day. Our reactions, however, won't be entirely in our immediate control. Our prehistoric stress response system will send us signals of panic – fight, flight or freeze – if we don't have the resources at that moment to cope with the stressor in our path.

The Yerkes-Dodson law
How stress affects performance.

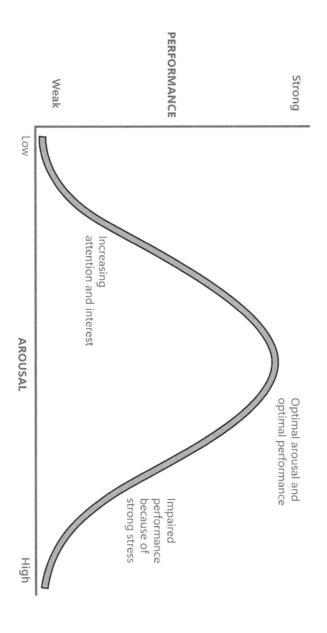

PERFORMANCE

Strong

Weak

AROUSAL

Low

High

Increasing attention and interest

Optimal arousal and optimal performance

Impaired performance because of strong stress

Imagine that your boss gives you a project and it is something you know you would enjoy. You have a good team around you, things are going well at home, and you've been looking after yourself well. Chances are you will relish the opportunity to do that project.

Now imagine you are given that project on a day when your best team member had resigned the day before. You had been to the pub to 'celebrate' with them where you had a few too many glasses of red wine and, finding yourself very hungry, had eaten a burger and chips on your way home. Not surprisingly, you didn't sleep well and woke up in a grotty mood which promptly kicked off a row with your partner. You arrive at work and that same project arrives on your desk.

The project is the project. Your reaction to it might be quite different though!

Every person is different in their reaction to pressure and how they manage stress. That's what makes managing stress at a management level so tricky.

Imagine I have a history of trauma, or that I was bullied in my last workplace, or I have a chronic health issue. Imagine that right now I am menopausal and dealing with adolescent young people and caring for my elderly dependants. Imagine that I am currently going through a relationship breakdown and have a history of leaning on alcohol to help me through.

For this reason, it can be difficult to separate work and home-related stress. Sometimes it can be wholly attributable to one or the other. Just as often, the two are intertwined.

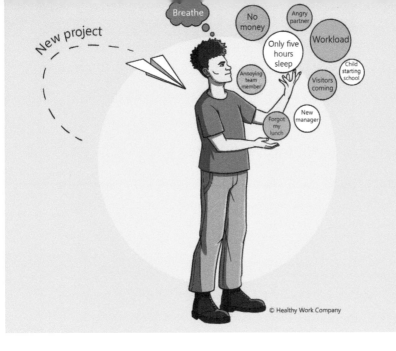

© Healthy Work Company

Outside of the fact that it is more difficult for us to impact someone's home life, as their manager, whether their stress is home- or work-related, we still end up dealing with the consequences.

We all have personal responsibility to look after ourselves (though I am absolutely clear that this is easier when we have help, are financially secure and can create the time – all of which are not the case for many people). But we are simply better able to cope with what life throws at us when we eat properly, don't self-medicate with drugs or alcohol, do some exercise, have a decent night's sleep, get some rest and surround ourselves with people who have our back.

Self-awareness and learning to self-regulate is important for human beings in this era.

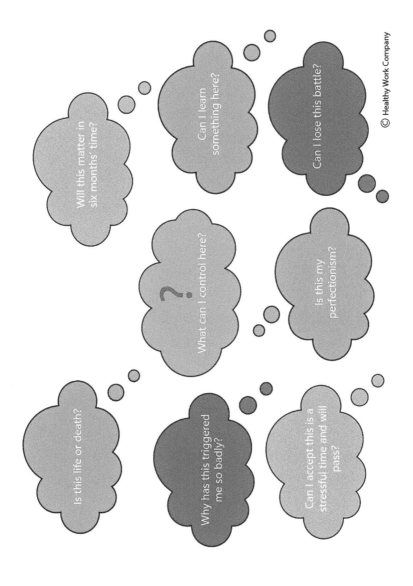

© Healthy Work Company

Our bodies communicate stress – through tight jaws or sickness, or just that feeling in your stomach or heart. We can't always logic our way out of it, despite having a pre-frontal cortex which allows us to reason. That reason is overridden when we are in a stress response.

Our bodies might need to tell the limbic system in the brain to calm down. We can do this by bringing our attention back to regularity and smoothness in our breathing or doing some physical exercise. Once we are back 'in the now' we can label that emotion – is it rage, frustration, humiliation, confusion? We can think about what is behind it, rationalise, take perspective. We can even try to reframe the stressful challenge and see it as positive.

Perspective might look like asking yourself, "Is this really life or death? Can I lose this particular argument? What value do I want to bring here? Could this be an opportunity for learning and growth?"

All of this speaks to the need for us to slow right down. This, however, is very difficult for those of us in straightened socioeconomic circumstances; those of us with caring responsibilities, or indeed those of us who have a habit of productivity, measure our worth through ticking things off our to-do list and thrive on being acknowledged for a job well done.

This image is based on Steven Covey's diagram which he based on the stoic philosophy that if we can't control an issue, we shouldn't worry about it. This approach is a very good tool for life stresses – can I control it? If not, can I at least influence it? Or, if it is completely outside of my control, can I reframe it?

WHERE DO YOU HAVE INFLUENCE AND CONTROL?

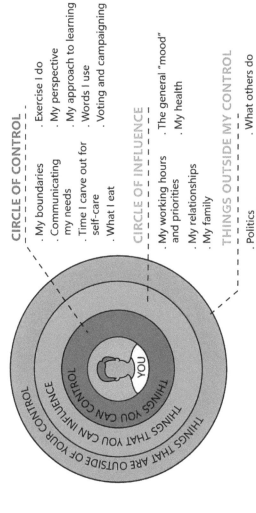

CIRCLE OF CONTROL

. My boundaries
. Communicating my needs
. Time I carve out for self-care
. What I eat

. Exercise I do
. My perspective
. My approach to learning
. Words I use
. Voting and campaigning

CIRCLE OF INFLUENCE

. My working hours and priorities
. My relationships
. My family

. The general "mood"
. My health

THINGS OUTSIDE MY CONTROL

. Politics
. The weather
. The economy
. What others think about me

. What others do and say
. Social media
. The news

THINGS YOU CAN CONTROL

THINGS THAT YOU CAN INFLUENCE

THINGS THAT ARE OUTSIDE OF YOUR CONTROL

YOU

Adapted from Steven Covey
"Seven Habits of Highly Effective People"
(1989)

Home or work?

Mostly in my employed working life I have had very good managers. I did however have a period which was truly awful. I returned from three years in Australia where I had nursed my failing marriage and had my daughter, Rosie. On return to the UK, I more or less immediately separated from my husband. With a two-year-old to care for, I went back to work four days a week in a business I had worked with before, in a less senior position at a lower salary. I was just about making ends meet, grieving for my marriage and dealing with a toddler whilst trying to do a five-day-week job in four days.

My boss, meantime, was younger than me, a new manager, less experienced in the business, insecure and was handling it (me!) badly. He would regularly invite everyone's opinion in a meeting aside from mine; he would talk over me and disagree with every proposal I made, at the same time exhausting me in one-to-ones by talking non-stop for hours.

I developed a throat infection, which meant I lost my voice. Then another, then another, then another. I was back and forth to the doctor who told me it was caused by stress.

Was this my home life or work life?

Regardless of whether it was home, work, or a mix of the two, the business suffered without my being at my productive, engaged best. For weeks I was too ill to work. That is bad for business.

Summary

- Pressure or challenge are good for us to a certain extent – but too much stress can lead us at best to underperform and at worst can make us ill.
- Our response to a stressor will be different according to our capacity at that particular moment in time.
- Human beings need to learn to self-regulate – which may include looking at stress-reduction techniques.

PART 3:
CREATING AN ENVIRONMENT
OF PSYCHOLOGICAL SAFETY

CHAPTER 6:

MANAGERS MATTER

People leave managers not companies.
Marcus Buckingham

There has been a big shift in understanding in most organisations that managers are integral to the creation of its culture. We already knew that 70 percent of team engagement was down to the manager[25] and, in a study released in February of 2023, the UK Workforce Group ascertained that for 69 percent of people, their manager had as great an impact on their mental health as their spouse[26].

As discussed above, workplaces are waking up to the fact that wellbeing can't be divorced from the overall management of the business. Senior level and middle managers need training in creating an environment in which people can thrive – from stress prevention strategies, to catching problems early when they arise, to managing an employee who needs further support.

If your wellbeing strategy is purely about raising awareness about mental health, about external interventions to support people when they are struggling and doesn't tackle management and culture, then it isn't a strategy.

Culture is 'how things are done around here'. As a manager or a leader, your ability to role model behaviours that promote good wellbeing, and to invest in conversations with your team that promote psychological safety, cannot be overestimated.

We have all worked for a terrible manager and for a great one and we know the difference that that person makes. Ironically, of course, most managers are not recruited or promoted for their management skills. Skills such as:

- Relationship management
- Communication and motivation
- Curiosity and listening
- Organisation and delegation
- Forward planning and strategic thinking
- Problem-solving and decision-making
- Commercial awareness

Instead, managers are often promoted because they are very good at the job they are doing. In fact, they are so good at it that, the next thing they know, they have a couple of people they are responsible for who are doing the job they used to do!

In general, in most countries, the best way of earning more, or of getting promoted, is to go into people management. Of course, if you are very good at engineering, or sales, or teaching, or nursing, or any number of other professions, it does not mean that you will have any of the management skills listed above.

Getting the right people managers in place has to be integral to your business strategy. We frequently work with organisations who aim to have a specific culture but, in reality, culture differs enormously from team to team. These micro-cultures are often driven by the team or the function manager.

A manager framework of expected behaviours should accompany the competencies required for the specific role. The framework needs to be lived and breathed – directing hiring, promotion and performance management. To understand your own workplace culture, ask the teams whether they are getting what they need from their managers. These 360-degree appraisals can be very confronting for managers but, for continuing self-awareness, they, or a tool like them, are key.

Psychological safety

Psychological safety is all about creating an environment where individuals feel free to express themselves and their ideas without fear of judgement or criticism.

This fosters healthy communication, collaboration and creative problem-solving, which can lead to better outcomes for everyone involved. When people are encouraged to challenge and argue in a safe space, it allows for innovation and new perspectives to emerge. This safe environment also encourages individuals to take risks and be vulnerable, which can lead to a greater sense of connection with others.

By fostering psychological safety, individuals are more likely to feel respected and valued, which can improve their mental health and overall wellbeing.

But it isn't just about being nice – it's also about being clear.

Clarity is an essential component of psychological safety because it helps to reduce ambiguity and provide a sense of security. When expectations and outcomes are crystal clear, individuals feel more confident in their ability to complete tasks and understand what is expected of them. This clarity helps to reduce confusion, build trust and foster collaboration and cooperation within a team or organisation. It also allows for better communication and problem-solving.

Create psychological safety by:

- Encouraging open communication
- Embracing vulnerability
- Practising respect and empathy
- Leading by example
- Clarifying expectations
- Encouraging healthy conflict
- Celebrating success

Role modelling as a manager and leader

Culture is 'how things are done around here'. The elevator conformity experiment featured on the American TV show Candid Camera[27] shows this in action. In this experiment we see how someone follows the crowd to understand what constitutes acceptable behaviour in a lift. As a manager or leader, you are very much responsible for 'how things are done around here'. Your team will look to you to see what acceptable behaviour is in this organisation.

Managers can role model good wellbeing in several ways:

1. Leading by example by taking regular breaks, exercising and eating healthy meals.
2. Encouraging employees to take breaks, get enough sleep and practise self-care.
3. Providing resources for employees who need help managing stress or mental health issues.
4. Promoting a culture of open communication and problem-solving. This may involve sharing some of their own vulnerabilities.
5. Setting a positive tone by being mindful of their own attitude and behaviour.
6. Allowing flexible work schedules and remote work options to promote work/life balance.
7. Creating a safe and comfortable work environment by setting clear expectations and boundaries.

Do all managers need to be able to have these conversations?

When Mental Health First Aid (a two-day course which trained people to notice the signs that a peer was struggling and refer them for further support) was first introduced, we heard from some organisations, "We don't need to train our managers, they can refer this conversation to a Mental Health First Aider if they can't handle it."

To be a manager of a team I think you do need to have a basic level of skill in this area and, at the very least, managers should not be referring these conversations to a more junior individual who has completed a two-day training course – a trained EAP counsellor or their HR team, perhaps.

In organisations where highly creative (sometimes difficult) people are in positions of power, they can be notorious for putting results high above people.

If you are in an industry where generally obnoxious leaders are tolerated because they get genius results, think about creating a structure where they are not responsible for people management. New matrix-managed structures can make this possible.

Finally, we hear people make assumptions that highly technical people are very bad at this.

Don't assume this. Often those of us with more extrovert personalities who think we are brilliant at communication, talk waaaaaay too much, give our advice and own experience liberally and overstep boundaries in our wish to 'help'.

Having trained thousands of people, my experience is that often those who are naturally more introverted are better at this. They are more reflective, ask good questions and know the boundaries.

Summary

- Research shows that managers have almost 70 percent impact on wellbeing and engagement.
- Explicit, desired manager behaviours should be made public in an organisation and regular feedback maintained.
- Creating an atmosphere of psychological safety is integral to wellbeing.
- As a manager, consider your role modelling – people look to you as the example of 'how things are done around here'.
- Having conversations about someone's wellbeing should be a basic manager competence.

CHAPTER 7:

SELF-KNOWLEDGE AND PERSONAL DEVELOPMENT

Know thyself
Socrates

How did you score yourself in 'self-knowledge' when you did our quiz at the beginning of the book? Are you someone who is really interested in why you do what you do, or is your view that all that is a bit self-indulgent?

Creating an environment in which challenge and pressure don't become overwhelm and stress, where people feel able to be themselves, where that elusive 'psychological safety' is present, requires us first and foremost as managers and leaders to master ourselves.

I just can't over-emphasise this.

When we are unconscious of our own stress, we take it out on others. When we don't understand our own triggers, we can find ourselves triggered by the actions or words of members of our team. When we aren't aware of our drivers, such as perfectionism, people pleasing, a desire to be loved, or imposter syndrome, we create a culture in the workplace where our team is treading lightly around our moods and emotions, whether we are aware of it or not.

First and most importantly, we need to understand ourselves and learn to self-regulate before we can be a really decent people manager.

We all know a boss who talks a good game, from the latest course or book they've read (let's hope not this one!), but underneath it you know that they will hijack all the conversations, or lose their temper, or drive their team into the ground. Not on purpose – they just aren't aware of the impact they are having or why they are doing what they are doing.

Self-knowledge and self-awareness

When you're always working on your self-awareness, you are developing a clearer understanding of your own strengths, weaknesses and biases.

This work is never done if you undertake it. Human beings are like onions – you peel one layer away and there is another underneath.

Many times in my life I have basked in a new set of self-knowledge and thought, "Ah yes, I am done now. My personal development journey has reached a new level"; only to find myself five years later, having run into a similar brick wall, with a different set of questions and a new set of insights. Generally, now I notice there is work to do because someone really makes me cross, or my body tells me through tight jaws or sickness.

Over time you might be able to start to recognise when you're feeling stressed or overwhelmed, and even (miracle of miracles!) to manage those emotions in a healthy way. And perhaps most importantly, you're able to open your mind to recognising when you're making mistakes, and you're willing to learn from them rather than shutting your eyes tightly and looking the other way because the knowledge is difficult.

The key for me is being able to face those things about ourselves which we would rather not know – to integrate them and make our peace with them. Then we can truly ask those questions of people, which we'd rather not know the answers to because they mean that we would have 'failed'. What could I do better? How can I behave differently to get the best out of you?

Blind spots

Even the most self-aware among us have blind spots and they will hold us back without us even realising. For example, maybe you tend to behave in an intimidating fashion, but you're unaware until you hear your nickname is 'bulldozer'.

Blind spots are, by definition, our unknown unknowns, So, how do we uncover them? Well, one of the best ways is to get some honest feedback! And here's the rub: when they tell you, don't get defensive! It can be really tempting to squirm inside, dwell on it, brush off negative feedback or make excuses for your behaviour, but that's not going to help you grow. Instead, try to really listen to what the other person is saying and see if there's anything you can learn from it.

Beware by the way, of someone who says they are 'fixed' and that they don't need to work on themselves any longer. This is **life-long work**.

Triggers

For most of my life I have found myself being highly judgemental about the behaviour of friends and colleagues. Then I read a book called *Owning Your Own Shadow*. In this book, Robert A Johnson explores the Jungian idea that we all have a shadow side to our personalities[28], which consists of those aspects of ourselves that we are not aware of, deny or repress. The premise of the book is that to become more whole and integrated individuals, we need to acknowledge and accept these shadow aspects of ourselves.

Over a couple of years, supported by the grief therapist who I picked as she had training in this shadow work, I realised that behind my judgements of others was fear of being judged myself. I believed I needed to be perfectly behaved or I would not be lovable. This cost me a few relationships before I realised it (in my fifties!), but it does now finally allow me to hear negative feedback about myself which I would have avoided at all costs before.

Shadow work

According to Jung, the shadow is the part of our psyche that contains all the aspects of ourselves that we have repressed or denied, either consciously or unconsciously. It's like the dark side of ourselves that we don't want to acknowledge or show to others. This can include our fears, insecurities, and even our desires and impulses that we consider inappropriate or shameful.

Shadow work is the process of exploring and integrating these repressed parts of ourselves. It's like shining a light into the darkness and bringing what's hidden into awareness.

The goal of shadow work is not to eliminate the shadow or become perfect, but rather to accept and integrate all aspects of ourselves. Jung believed that by acknowledging and embracing our shadow, we can become more authentic and whole individuals. It's like the saying, "What you resist, persists".

By confronting our shadow, we can let go of the power it holds over us and find greater peace and freedom in our lives.

Johari window

The Johari window consists of a four-quadrant model that helps individuals understand their relationship with themselves and others. The model is based on the idea that there are aspects of ourselves that are known to us and others, and aspects that are unknown to both. By identifying and understanding these different areas, individuals can improve their communication, build stronger relationships, and enhance their personal growth.

The Johari Window Model

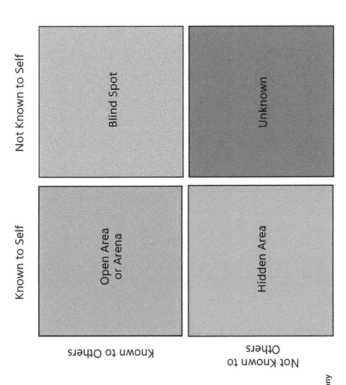

Known to Self   Not Known to Self

Known to Others

Open Area or Arena

Blind Spot

Not Known to Others

Hidden Area

Unknown

Insecurity

Most of us suffer from this at some point in our lives and some will never get through it. We may be aware of it, or it may be one of those notorious blind spots.

It can be incredibly destructive as a manager when we, as we so often do, take it out on those around us. We might be worried about someone in our team taking our job, so constantly feel we have to show how great we are or take all the credit for a project. On the other hand, we may feel that someone's performance won't show us in the best light, so we micromanage them.

Insecurity stems from our own personal history and experiences. Perhaps we felt we had to be a certain way to be accepted or were criticised or belittled or our achievements never acknowledged. Maybe we've had past experiences that have left us feeling hurt, rejected, or unworthy. These experiences can all contribute to feelings of insecurity that persist long into adulthood.

Lack of emotion regulation

Emotion regulation is all about managing our feelings and emotions in a healthy and adaptive way. When we're able to regulate our emotions effectively, we can respond to situations in a way that's appropriate and helpful, rather than just reacting impulsively.

We have all been in a situation where we felt really angry or upset and sent that email we later regretted! That is an example of poor emotion regulation. When we're able to regulate our emotions effectively, we're better able to cope with stress, manage conflicts, and maintain healthy relationships. Emotion regulation can involve a variety of strategies, such as deep breathing, mindfulness, positive self-talk, and learning to recognise and manage our triggers so that we're less likely to get swept up in strong emotions.

Perfectionism

Perfectionism is one I know all too well. **And** it's one I only recently identified as something which has run me my whole life. It serves us to a certain extent, that striving for excellence, but it can also be a source of stress, anxiety and burnout. Those of us who have perfectionist traits struggle to delegate. We may have unrealistic expectations for ourselves and others and feel the need to always operate at our full potential.

According to Kristen Neff[29], a primary researcher in the field of self-compassion, perfectionism is often driven by a fear of failure or a need for approval. Perfectionists tend to set impossibly high standards for themselves and feel anxious or guilty if they don't meet those standards.

Three types of perfectionism

Hewitt, Flett and Frost are key researchers in the field of perfectionism. They have identified three types of perfectionism[30].

• Self-oriented perfectionism: Having very high standards for yourself and expecting yourself to operate at those standards all the time. High achievement is likely, of course, but can lead so easily to burnout and excessive self-criticism.

• Other-oriented perfectionism: Expecting those same high standards from others at all times, not respecting those who don't try to better themselves. This kind of perfectionism makes you stressful to work with and makes you judgemental of others.

• Socially-prescribed perfectionism: This is where you feel external pressure to be perfect, such as from family, peers, or society.

Self-compassion

Absolutely no one is perfect – and would we want to live in a world where they were? Embracing our imperfections, recognising that imperfection is a natural part of the human experience allows us to practise self-compassion. If you are someone (like I was) who speaks to themselves as if they were their own worst enemy ('you idiot'), try speaking to yourself as you would your best friend.

The practice of being self-compassionate has an unforeseen benefit. By working on our ability to forgive and accept ourselves, we can also more easily forgive and accept the mistakes of others.

Becoming more self-aware

If, having read this, you are committed to getting to know yourself better and to integrate those things you don't particularly like about yourself, here are some good ways to gain greater self-awareness.

1. Be open to feedback: Seek out feedback from others, including your team members, peers, and superiors, and be willing to listen to what they have to say.
2. Seek out diverse perspectives and experiences: This can help you to challenge (and realise!) your own biases and assumptions and gain a broader understanding of the world around you. Talk to people who have different backgrounds, beliefs, and experiences, and be open to learning from them.

3. Get a mentor, coach or therapist: A mentor or coach will guide you and can help you identify your strengths and weaknesses; a therapist might help you understand yourself better and may take the sting out of some of your perceived weaknesses by creating a safe place.

4. Identify your triggers: Take time to reflect on what triggers strong emotional reactions in you. Is it criticism, conflict, uncertainty or something else? Once you've identified your triggers, you can develop strategies for managing your emotions when you encounter them.

5. Practise the listening skills in this book: Active listening is a skill that can help you to become more self-aware. When you're engaging in conversation with others, make a conscious effort to really listen to what they're saying. This will also help you to build stronger relationships.

Summary

- Self-awareness is absolutely fundamental to being a good manager, along with being willing to seek honest feedback.
- Self-awareness is not an overnight thing, but an ongoing life-long journey and we need to find ways to open up our blind spots (unknown unknowns).
- Insecurity, lack of emotion regulation and perfectionism are key difficulties for managers which will really impede their team. However, antidotes to this are shadow work and self-compassion.

CHAPTER 8:

THE IMPORTANCE OF SELF-CARE AS A MANAGER

A joyful life is an individual creation that cannot be copied from a recipe.
Mihaly Csikszentmihalyi

Prioritising **rest, exercise, sleep and breaks** is very hard in the modern world where we judge ourselves by our productivity levels, where we are constantly 'on call' and where many of us have very high standards for our work. It can be even harder when we have responsibilities for others in our team and where we feel that our work is so fulfilling that it is almost like play. (I'm speaking for myself here – I have learnt that it may feel like it, but I do need to change it up a bit!)

We've all heard the expressions, "You can't pour from an empty cup" and "Put your own oxygen mask on before you help anyone else". As we have seen from this book, managers are under increasing pressure not only as human beings (as we all are) but from the increasing complexity in managing their team.

Speaking for myself, I know that the more time I spend on the hamster wheel of work without taking a proper break, the more I am unable to see other possibilities. It impedes my creativity, judgement and capacity for self-reflection.

The mini business case for looking after ourselves is simply that we can then cope with more stressors when we get back to work. And, as we look after ourselves, this will give others permission to do the same.

I operate by working very hard and then taking a complete break every two to three months. Every year I think creating everyday balance will get easier, and it never seems to. At the moment I think my strategy works, but no doubt there is another layer of the onion to peel!

Here are just a few of the benefits of taking care of yourself as a manager:

- Burnout prevention: The benefits of physical exercise to close off the stress cycle can't be underestimated. Other short cuts are those activities which stimulate the Vagus nerve.
- Better decision-making, creativity and productivity.
- Role modelling: Culturally we play a huge role in giving others permission to rest if we rest too.
- We won't take our stress out on those in the team.

Remember that whilst there is scientific evidence for the effectiveness of certain self-care practices, we are all different.

PILLARS OF WELLBEING

| Good Nutrition | Exercise | Sleep | Rest and Relaxation | Manage your Thinking | Human Connection |

Csikszentmihalyi's quote, "A joyful life is an individual creation that cannot be copied from a recipe"[31] is in line with his belief that the key to happiness and wellbeing is not a one-size-fits-all approach, but rather a unique set of experiences and activities that are meaningful to the individual. We must engage in activities that bring us a sense of purpose and flow, and that allow us to use our unique skills and talents to create a joyful and fulfilling life.

Managing our wellbeing

Good nutrition

The gut-brain axis is a complex connection and research has shown that the health of the gut can influence mood, anxiety and cognitive function. Cooking from scratch, eating a wide range of fruit and vegetables and including fermented food such as sauerkraut and kefir in your diet can be really helpful, as well as avoiding too much alcohol and heavily processed food.

Exercise

Incorporating exercise into your daily routine can significantly improve your mental health. Exercise releases endorphins, which are natural feel-good chemicals that can help reduce symptoms of anxiety and depression and increase feelings of happiness and wellbeing. Physical activity can also reduce stress by decreasing the production of cortisol, a stress hormone. Regular exercise can improve quality of sleep, boost self-esteem and confidence, and provide a sense of accomplishment. Whether it is going to the gym or simply getting off the bus early and using the stairs at work, incorporating it into your daily routine can have significant mental health benefits.

Sleep

Most of us need between seven to nine hours sleep a night for optimum functioning. During sleep, the brain consolidates and processes information, and restores and repairs tissues throughout the body. Getting adequate sleep also supports the immune system, helps regulate hormones and can improve mood and cognitive function. Without enough sleep, individuals may experience increased irritability, difficulty concentrating, and impaired decision-making abilities.

Rest and relaxation

In the modern world it is very hard to get enough rest and there are many types which can be beneficial.

- Taking breaks throughout the day, such as stretching or going for a walk, can help reduce stress and increase productivity.
- Mental rest, such as meditation or deep breathing exercises, can also be beneficial for mental health by reducing anxiety and promoting relaxation.

- Social rest, such as spending time with loved ones or engaging in hobbies, can help reduce feelings of loneliness and improve mood.
- Sensory rest, such as reducing exposure to noise and bright lights, can help promote relaxation and improve the quality of sleep.
- Active rest may include the cultivation of hobbies which totally absorb you and promote 'flow'.

Manage your thinking

Your thoughts are not the truth. Re-read that! Our brains are sense-making machines and we draw immediate conclusions from what happens, creating a story round it. We need to recognise that for the story it is and then look at whether it empowers us or whether it does not. If it doesn't (which, with our inbuilt negativity bias, it often won't) then we can create a new interpretation. Being aware of our thoughts is critical here – we can do this by speaking them aloud or writing them down.

Human connection

Even the most introverted among us need a level of connection with others. Human connection can provide us with a sense of belonging, and feeling connected to others can promote feelings of happiness, reduce stress, and improve overall quality of life.

The nervous system

Have you ever wondered about the trend for ice baths or open water swimming?

The power of this activity is that it activates the vagus nerve which is a key part of our parasympathetic nervous system. The parasympathetic nervous system works in contrast to the sympathetic nervous system, which activates the body's 'fight or flight' response to stressors. By stimulating the vagus nerve, we can promote the activation of the parasympathetic nervous system, leading to feelings of relaxation and reducing the negative effects of stress on the body.

Key ways to activate the nerve include:

1. Deep breathing exercises, including diaphragmatic breathing and alternate nostril breathing

2. Yoga and gentle exercise, including walking, swimming and tai chi
3. Meditation and mindfulness practices
4. Cold exposure, including splashing cold water on the face, taking cold showers or immersing the face/body in ice water
5. Gargling or humming
6. Acupuncture
7. Massage therapy and reflexology
8. Chanting or singing
9. Walking barefoot on the earth
10. Laughter

The new science of positive psychology

The science of positive psychology is also researching interventions that make a difference to our ability to be well and happy. The areas currently being researched include:

1. Gratitude: If we are on the lookout for what to be grateful for in our everyday life we will gradually notice more things to be grateful for. It is thought that practising gratitude literally rewires our brain for greater happiness and life satisfaction.
2. Mindfulness: Mindfulness interventions, such as meditation or yoga, have been shown to reduce stress and anxiety, increase positive emotions and improve overall wellbeing. We know that bringing regularity

and smoothness to our breath enables us to soothe our stress response system, but just taking frequent moments to be present, to savour a view, to feel our feet on the floor all help to bring us back to 'now'.

3. Positive emotions: Seeking joy, contentment and amusement have been linked to increased wellbeing and happiness.

4. Strengths and values: Identifying and utilising one's strengths and values can lead to being in 'flow' which brings both in-the-moment happiness and long-term life satisfaction. This one is strongly linked to the work we choose to do.

5. Savouring: Being mindful and present in the moment to fully appreciate positive experiences.

6. Spirituality: A sense of connection to something greater than oneself and can include practices such as meditation, prayer or engaging in religious or spiritual practices.

7. Positive thinking: Focusing on positive aspects of oneself, others and the world, and can include practices such as reframing negative experiences or practising positive self-talk.

8. Forgiveness: Letting go of anger, resentment or negative emotions towards oneself or others.

9. Resilience: The ability to maintain a positive outlook in the face of challenges. Resilience interventions, such as building social support networks or developing problem-solving skills, have been shown to increase wellbeing and happiness.

Summary

- It can be really hard to prioritise looking after ourselves when we are on the hamster wheel of productivity or have real and huge demands on our time. However, understanding what makes us happy and brings us increased energy, and putting a proactive plan in place to look after ourselves, will absolutely benefit our work and those around us.
- By looking after yourself as a manager, you give those around you permission to do the same.
- There are many different ways to look after our physical and mental health including, but not limited to, exercise, sleep, rest, nutrition, managing our thinking, and human connection.
- Every single human being will require different ingredients to create a happy life – the ideas in this chapter are science-driven but pick those which most appeal to you.

PART 4:
HAVING
"THE CONVERSATION"

CHAPTER 9:

A STRUCTURE FOR "THAT CONVERSATION"

*Listening well means being present, open and curious,
and making the other person feel heard and accepted.*
Julian Treasure

However good a manager you are, at some point you will be faced with a conversation with someone struggling. As we have seen in Part 2: "Understanding mental health, wellbeing and stress", we are in difficult times and whether it is a home or work problem, we need to be equipped to deal with it.

How often do we notice someone is struggling, or suspect they might be and just hope it will go away? Perhaps we are brave enough to start that conversation but then we overshare, or problem solve or give advice.

I spent a full year honing my listening skills on a personal development programme which examined what I was bringing at the time to each 'difficult' conversation – often fear, trepidation and a fully pre-conceived idea of who that person was and how the conversation would go.

Having built our courses, we came up with this mnemonic for which I credit my ex-colleague Lauren Applebey.

This is in use in hundreds of organisations and is integrated into Highfield Qualifications mental health courses too.

Of course, this can never be an entirely stepped- and mapped-out process. A conversation isn't a precise science but more of a dance. I notice this no more than when we bring our training alive using forum theatre. Our actors are masters at changing the parameters, reacting in a way which feels true to them, and which emulates the very real challenges managers face when dealing with someone struggling.

But this is great for people to observe (and participate if they want to). The more we practise and think about how we did, the better we can get at this.

Forum theatre

Forum theatre is a training technique, using actors, which brings alive a conversation in the workplace so that participants can witness common mistakes for themselves. In this case, in reviewing the conversation, participants coach the 'manager' (actor) to change their tone, words and body language. We create a script consistent with one of your specific workplace challenges.

It is always better to be aware and to ask than to bury your head in the sand. A problem caught early may not develop into a huge issue. Most humans need to be listened to and acknowledged first and foremost. You don't actually need to say as much as you think you do and you can always say, "I will need to go away and think about this" rather than having to have answers there and then.

A   **Awareness** then Approach, Ask, Assess

B   **Be Present,** Listen and Support

C   **Co-create a Plan,** Work out Next Steps Together

D   **Your Duties** under HR and H&S Law

© Healthy Work Company

Suppose they don't want to talk to me?

We are often asked, supposing someone doesn't want to talk about it? Or, they say things are fine again and again (and then fall over).

That is sometimes the case.

You can't force someone to talk about something if they feel it is their personal business and they don't want to share it. They might not be ready to talk about it or maybe can't recognise what you are talking about. They might not want to speak specifically to you – perhaps, God forbid, you are part of the problem!

However, you can leave the door open. Ask if there is anyone else they would prefer to talk to; check back in a week or so if your concern persists; say, "I am here if you do want to talk."

Critically, of course, as you are this individual's manager and if their performance is part of the problem or their behaviour in the team is causing issues, you may need to persist – but you still can't force them to tell you what is going on. Think about being really clear about the performance issue and ask what support you can provide – either personally or from the organisation – in order to see an improvement in that area.

Finally, if we focus our energy on stress prevention by asking regularly whether someone has the resources to do everything they have on at the time and creating an environment in which they can safely say when that isn't the case (psychological safety), we may find this situation happens less frequently.

I'm a boss, not a shrink

The premise of this book is 'I'm a boss, not a shrink'.

Let's dig into that.

There are obviously **HUGE** differences in the role of therapist and boss.

Therapists are educated and trained in understanding human psychology and supporting individuals to understand themselves better, to be well and to be happier. They are often trained in in many modalities.

Some of the modalities in therapy

1. Cognitive Behavioural Therapy (CBT): identifying and changing negative patterns of thinking and behaviour that contribute to mental health problems.
2. Psychodynamic Therapy: how early life experiences and unconscious thoughts and feelings impact current behaviours and relationships.
3. Humanistic Therapy: the importance of personal growth and self-actualisation. This focuses on the client's individual experience and perspective.
4. Family Systems Therapy: Looks at the ways in which family dynamics and interactions impact individuals and seeks to improve communication and relationships within the family.
5. Mindfulness-based Therapy: practices to help clients become more aware of their thoughts and emotions and learn to manage them more effectively.

6. Dialectical Behaviour Therapy (DBT): a type of CBT that focuses specifically on managing emotions and developing skills for regulating intense or difficult emotions.
7. Acceptance and Commitment Therapy (ACT): helping clients accept their thoughts and feelings without judgement and develop values-based goals and actions.

Therapists will be acute observers of language, both verbal and bodily expressed. They will deeply understand the signs of not just distress but of mental illnesses and be able to say when they know that this particular issue is not within their expertise.

Therapists have to do ongoing CPD and are constantly evolving their education.

Therapy is a regulated profession with governance inside different professional bodies. It is supervised so you not only have to have your own therapy but discuss cases with your supervisor.

Now let's compare a therapist with a manager.

Managers are typically focused on achieving measurable outcomes and maintaining operational efficiency. They do this through getting the best out of their people and in theory their primary role is to coach and lead, not 'do'. Yet most managers do not have their day job taken away when they are made a manager and have had very little or no training in using other people to get the job done. They are told to coach without being shown how.

Let's also contrast the power relationship.

I can say whatever I want to my therapist – it is a completely safe environment, and they should be unshockable.

My boss however, lovely as they may be, has the power to remove my income from me.

Your therapist is there to serve you and you alone. Your manager, however, needs to serve the needs of the people **and** the needs of the business.

What can managers learn from therapists and coaches?

Therapists and managers **should** both be good listeners. A therapist would be hopeless if they were not brilliant at this. Both, to a certain extent, can employ active listening techniques which encourage the person struggling to find their own solutions.

Can you be a good manager without being a good listener?

In the command-and-control environment in which we used to operate, managers got away with just telling people to get on with it. Now we see increasing cultures of collaboration which rely on good listening. In very hierarchical cultures around the world, often there will be complex, shared, collaborative decision-making models (which may be invisible to someone from another part of the world!)

Is it only a more recent perspective to think that a skill for good listening is a quality which marks out a good human? Perhaps certain parts of the population (those in charge) didn't always feel the need to listen in the past. But now that the social contract is up for negotiation, in my view, we all must learn to listen better.

(Sadly, even those who think of ourselves as good listeners are often incapable of hearing someone out where we profoundly disagree. But that is another story.)

Another thing managers and therapists **should** have in common is boundaries.

In the therapist case, those are strictly enforced and super easy to see. Their service is time limited – usually to a regular hour. It is possible to get emergency support with some, but that is time you pay for, and some will flat out say 'no' and suggest you call your doctor or the Samaritans.

In the manager case, whilst boundaries are critical, they are much, much less clear and more difficult to enforce. It can be really hard as a manager to enforce boundaries. Workplaces often have the feeling of being a family (especially where they are indeed family-owned businesses). If you look at the field of Transactional Analysis, we can become parental as a manager and our 'charges' become our 'children'.

We need to regularly pose ourselves the question. Do I have capacity to help right now, how much can I realistically offer, and am I the best person to support this individual?

What is Transactional Analysis

Transactional Analysis (TA) is a psychoanalytic theory and therapy approach developed by Eric Berne in the 1950s. It is based on the idea that individuals have three ego states – parent, adult, and child – that are each characterised by distinct patterns of behaviour, thoughts and feelings.

In the workplace, individuals may adopt a 'parent' ego state, where they take on a role of authority and may act in a controlling or directive manner towards others. Alternatively, they may adopt a 'child' ego state, where they may act in a dependent or rebellious manner and may require a high degree of guidance and support.

However, it is important to note that TA does not suggest that individuals are always in one ego state or another. Rather, individuals can move between ego states depending on the situation, their mood, and other factors.

Overall, the application of TA in the workplace is not about labelling individuals as one ego state or another, but rather about developing greater self-awareness and effective communication skills to improve relationships and performance.

Summary

- Both managers and therapists need excellent listening skills and, to a certain extent, an understanding that human beings often hold their own solutions.
- Therapists have ongoing training and CPD and it is a regulated profession; managers may have little or no training in being a manager or in listening skills.
- It is much easier to hold boundaries as a therapist. As a manager this is not always clearly set out.

CHAPTER 10:

COMMON PITFALLS

*Kindness and intelligence don't always deliver us
from the pitfalls and traps: there are always failures
of love, of will, of imagination. There is no way to
take the danger out of human relationships.*
Barbara Grizzuti Harrison

Aside from the very real human desire to fix and solve which might lead us to present 'solutions' to an individual too early on in the conversation, there are some other common traps which we may as managers fall into.

A lack of boundaries

Unlike a therapist, manager boundaries are not clear. Some organisations prefer their managers to be very human and to bend over backwards to support individuals to the point of almost operating *in loco parentis*. Others will want to maintain some professionalism and boundaries. I have seen both approaches in two cases at two different organisations with an employee's attempted suicide.

Organisation one: HR were horrified to find the manager at the employee's bedside in hospital twice in two days, also talking to the family of the individual. They felt that this behaviour displayed a complete lack of boundaries and that this should be dealt with by more formal support mechanisms.

Organisation two: MD personally accompanied someone they had very real mental health concerns about to the doctor and then spoke to them every day for weeks even when in hospital – at weekends, in the evenings.

I don't know where I sit on this. I think probably in the camp of those who lost the boundaries, but it is a legitimate question to ask ourselves regularly.

In our desire to help and support an individual, we may bend over backwards to support someone, often at high cost to ourselves or the rest of the team. We should ask ourselves: is this fair to everyone else? Who out of all these should I and can I help? To whom do I make my time available?

It is so tempting to say, "Come and see me any time, my door is always open, call me whenever you need to – evenings, weekends…" Ultimately that is your choice and perhaps this was manageable when you had one case every year or two, but is this really a sustainable strategy now or is it at too great a cost to you and your own life? More importantly, are you doing that person a service? This is hugely difficult. Showing you care can be integral to their recovery. Not making that care appear transactional and cold but at the same time recognising the limits of your expertise and resources is the difficult art you must master.

Remember the extent of your own expertise, your role

and the fact that you are not a mental health professional. Can you instead focus on listening to their concerns and offering referrals or resources as needed?

I have had multiple experiences in training of managers saying they feel that they are permanently on call for an individual struggling with a mental health issue and they don't know what to say or how to handle this.

Consider saying something like, *"This is just not my area of expertise. I really want to support you, but I would be doing you a disservice if I didn't suggest you talk to someone who really does know what they are talking about. Did you call the number I gave you last time?"* Organisations who espouse a culture of 'bring your whole self to work' also need to consider where the boundaries are. Is it acceptable to turn up in your pyjamas or to regularly have emotional outbursts? This new world opens up all sorts of questions we need to examine.

Governance of Mental Health First Aid programmes

Whilst this is a book for managers, we are aware that many managers were initially trained as Mental Health First Aiders in spite of the fact that follow up with an individual is a different matter as a manager.

In more recent times, for Mental Health First Aid in the UK, programme governance has had much greater consideration. You should, in fact, not only set out a role description for a Mental Health First Aider and define the support you are offering those that take the role, but also ensure that managers and HR people who go through the course are clear on which hat they are wearing when they have a conversation with someone struggling. It should be clearly stated that, in general, their duties as a manager/HR person trump those of Mental Health First Aider. In essence though, my suggestion is that managers and HR people should do a course which is fit for purpose for their own duties as well as, or instead of, a Mental Health First Aid-type course.

Then, you need to set a context for boundaries when it comes to ongoing support of an individual. We have found organisations have different points of view here!

- **Organisation one:** HR client one was horrified to find that Mental Health First Aiders were booking a room and telling people they would be in it to conduct Mental Health conversations one day a month and finding people coming back again and again.
- **Organisation two:** HR client two was congratulating themselves on creating an ongoing support hub in a room where there was coffee served every week and where people could discuss their mental health issues with Mental Health First Aiders who chose to attend.

Who is right?

These are the knotty issues which Mental Health First Aid programmes have thrown up and which we talk clients through. Remember that your Mental Health First Aiders are not professionally trained counsellors, therapists or life coaches. They also have a day job to do.

Note that, at the time of writing, there is no legal requirement anywhere in the world to have a Mental Health First Aider, but it can work well to build internal awareness. However, some of our clients make the proactive choice not to introduce this programme. Instead, they might offer a short course to train everyone who wants to improve their skillset in having mental health conversations – we call these 'Better Wellbeing Conversations'. This approach democratises a skillset which we could all improve on and doesn't make it the special skillset of a small number of individuals. We train in both – an internationally applicable version of Mental Health First Aid, tailored to the organisation and co-written with Highfield Qualifications, or a short 'Conversations for Wellbeing' course.

Failing to follow up

Once you've had a wellbeing conversation with an employee, it's important to follow up and confirm what you agreed and then check in with them to see how they're doing. Failing to follow up can send the message that you don't care or that their concerns aren't important.

Over empathising

As a manager, it's important to be empathetic and supportive when employees are struggling. Over empathising can sometimes be counterproductive, however. It can lead to your own emotional burnout, a dependency from the individual on you and set unrealistic expectations in terms of your ability to provide ongoing emotional support. It can even lead to enabling unhealthy behaviours. For example, if the manager is too permissive or accommodating, the individual may not feel motivated to seek out appropriate treatment or make the changes they need to manage their mental health effectively.

We are not machines and we may, on occasion, feel very impacted by someone's issues. But does this make us a better person or a better support?

Sometimes we may project our own fears and uncertainties and feel sympathetic in a way which doesn't actually support the person – perhaps that individual may welcome a more pragmatic approach which makes the issue seem smaller and you stepping in with your own tears may not be what they need.

Friendships with people in your team

It's hard to avoid the fact that you may feel naturally drawn to certain people and have friendships which may pre-date your manager role. You do need to treat everyone equally and fairly, whether they are your friends or not. Be objective in your decision-making and set clear expectations for everyone. You need to focus on building relationships with all members of your team, not just your friends – and at all costs avoid gossip. Gossiping with your friends about other team members or discussing work-related matters outside of work can create the perception of favouritism and erode trust within the team.

Summary

- Key pitfalls when it comes to wellbeing conversations would be a lack of boundaries (which are difficult to establish!), failing to follow up, over empathising and unequal treatment due to friendships with members of the team.
- Be aware that if you bring a Mental Health First Aid programme in, you need to consider the governance issues.

CHAPTER 11:

A FOR AWARENESS, APPROACH, ASK, ASSESS

The whole idea of compassion is based on a keen awareness of the interdependence of all these living beings, which are all part of one another, and all involved in one another.
Thomas Merton

Aware that there is a problem...

The first thing is to notice that the individual is struggling. This has become harder with the growth of hybrid and remote work. Most of the signs which you can pick up face to face, you can also pick up when someone is on a screen with you or on the phone, but it is just not so easy to see if there is a consistent problem – because you are not seeing them all day.

Notice, with the exception of burnout – which is regarded as an occupational condition – we don't try to break the 'signs and symptoms' down into different types of mental illness. Our job as managers is not to attempt to diagnose – just to notice someone is struggling.

Many of our delegates, indeed you may have answered positively to this question in our quiz, instinctively **know** most of the obvious signs that someone is struggling, which we have laid out below. But it is sometimes the oddest things which are worth asking about: my team member 'P' with his rashes, my own continuous throat infections, an early team member with persistent hair loss.

1. Decreased productivity or quality of work: They may find it difficult to concentrate, stay focused, and complete tasks on time. They may also make more mistakes than usual.

2. Increased absence or lateness: They may find it difficult to get out of bed in the morning or may feel too overwhelmed to come to work. They may also take more sick days than usual – remember that connection between physical and mental health.

3. Changes in behaviour or mood: This is a key one to look for. We all know that some people are naturally quieter than others, but you are looking for changes. Those who normally take things in their stride becoming more irritable, anxious, or more withdrawn than usual. People who are normally noisy, going quiet. They may also have mood swings or seem more emotional – ranging from tearful to angry.

4. Presenteeism: Working late all the time, not taking holidays, being at work when they should be off sick (and hence not performing well either).

SPOTTING THE SIGNS OF SOMEONE STRUGGLING

Decreased productivity or quality of work

Absence, lateness, turning camera off

Increased substance or alcohol use

Presenteeism

Changes in behaviour or mood

Change in physical appearance

Emotional or easily triggered

Someone else might tell you

5. Substance use: People who are struggling with their mental health may turn to alcohol or drugs to cope with their feelings.

6. Changes in physical appearance: Looking tired, unkempt, presenting with poor hygiene or a change in the way they dress. Face to face this may be easier to establish especially if you are looking for signs of self-harm or an eating disorder.

7. They don't turn up or turn off their camera: If you are working purely online with them, they may not show up for meetings or they may have their camera off. You may see cryptic statements on social media.

8. Someone else tells you! Often a colleague will notice something is 'off' before you do and draw it to your attention.

Risk assessing for burnout

Burnout is included in the eleventh revision of the WHO's International Classification of Diseases as a syndrome resulting from chronic workplace stress that has not been successfully managed – and it is a key risk for businesses today.

In many countries in Europe it has been recognised by doctors for some time and in the UK many healthcare professionals are now being trained in recognising it – in their own profession too.

Whilst we may blame workplaces for creating an environment where people burn out, we need to go back to the diagram we saw in Chapter 3 (see page 47) and remind ourselves that there is an interplay between the organisation, the manager and the individual.

I experienced burnout when working for myself. The organisation was my own and I had no manager. I enjoyed work so much that it could be tempting to see it as play and not to recognise that I needed to use other types of rest!

Burnout can manifest as feelings of exhaustion, detachment, and cynicism towards work or personal relationships. You may find someone is increasingly irritable, anxious, or depressed and may struggle to concentrate or make decisions. Physical symptoms of burnout can include headaches, stomach aches, and sleep disturbances.

Its manifestation in me was that I stopped believing I could make a difference; I found my work pointless; I got increasingly fatigued and then one day I just couldn't get out of bed. Recovery involved a complete break and focusing on my nutrition and exercise. I was lucky. My burnout only lasted a few weeks.

Getting to know your team

In these days of remote and hybrid working, we need to think much more proactively about:

- Regular check-ins: Set up regular one-on-one check-ins with remote workers to discuss their work, projects, and any challenges they may be facing.
- Virtual coffee chats: Try to emulate those informal conversations which help you get to know them better.

- Virtual team building activities: Online games, virtual happy hours or group exercises to help remote workers connect with each other and build relationships. (Do be sensitive that these are not everyone's cup of tea!)
- Mind Wellness Action plans: These are a structure for a conversation you can have together (if relationships allow) or individually with each member of your team to ask how they like to be managed and what they find stressful.

Approaching

It can be very tempting to plan everything in advance for this conversation – to go in considering what they might say and what you might say back, and what ideas you have for their supposed problem. In reality, there are three things to prepare:

- Yourself: Are you in the right frame of mind to have this conversation? Should you go and mentally prepare yourself by doing some breathing exercises or talking to someone first?
- Some examples: Of what you have noticed
- Your approach: Where, when and how

Let's look at considerations for where and when.

1. How urgently do you think you need to talk to them? Perhaps normalise tackling what you notice sooner rather than later.

2. Make sure you actually have time for the conversation. If someone approaches for a conversation and you are about to start a meeting, you may need to make a snap judgement about the urgency of their need and either duck out of the meeting or schedule the conversation for when you do have a proper gap in your diary.

3. Are you seeing them face-to-face soon? Can you take them for coffee? It is much easier to have these conversations side-by-side or walking. Perhaps if you are not seeing them you could suggest you both speak on a walking meeting on the phone? If you are seeing them face-to-face, try not to sit directly opposite them.

4. Is the screen a suitable medium for that person to have a difficult conversation with you? Online they are required to stare you directly in the face. Whilst we know that we can pick up a lot from body language which will be missing on the phone, counterintuitively, some people will respond more easily this way.

5. Don't entirely dismiss text to start with. Especially when approaching younger generations, they may be much more open on text than they will be face-to-face. As someone's manager I certainly don't think text is the only medium in which you should be talking to them, but it can be a good way to check in on someone struggling.

Asking

We got so much better during the pandemic at asking how someone was in a way which showed that we were genuinely interested in the answer. Perhaps we shared a vulnerability or asked, "How are you really?" or enquired about a difficulty we knew they were having. We might even have said something like, "On a scale of one to ten, with one being terrible and ten being great, how are you today?" For a while we took off our armour of capability. Is this an art we are now losing in a maelstrom of more hard work?

The more we check in, in a genuinely interested way, the easier it will be to address signs we think someone may be struggling when we notice them.

How we do that will depend on how well we know that individual and how **they** like to be spoken to. One of my best bosses, Millsy (Simon Mills), knew I was very direct and so he would take me into a meeting room and say, "Beach, what's going on? You're not yourself." He would not replicate that with the more introverted, quieter members of the team where he would lead up to it gently and couch it sensitively.

A mistake we can make though is just hoping that if we do enough small talk that it will eventually come up in the conversation. The problem with this approach is that the subtext of the conversation will be clear from the start, and they will be waiting for you to say what you need to say.

Practise normalising saying such things as "You didn't seem yourself on that call, you are normally really interactive, and you were so quiet today, is there anything going on you want to share?" or "That piece of work just wasn't like you. I normally get something absolutely brilliant, and this had X, Y and Z missing. Did I brief you badly or is there something else I should know about?"

Cultural sensitivities when managing a global team

As outlined in the Introduction, under the heading 'International applicability', we do have to think about the assumptions we are bringing to conversations when we are managing someone from a different culture and think they may be struggling with a wellbeing issue or life struggle. Mental health stigma can vary across cultures. In some cultures, mental health issues may be seen as a personal weakness or something to be ashamed of.

Communication styles can also vary across cultures. Some cultures may be more indirect or less likely to speak up about mental health issues. Adapting your communication style to the cultural norms of the other person can help build rapport and facilitate effective communication. This may involve adjusting your tone, pace, or choice of words to better match the other person's communication style.

Educating yourself about cultural norms where your team member lives will be helpful here. A great book, which you can find in Resources section at the back of this book, is Erin Meyer's *The Culture Map*.

At a recent international Mental Health First Aid course, we had a case study where the person in the study had been using suicidal language. When feeding back from the discussions about how they would approach this, there was a marked difference between the Indian and the British groups. The British preferred to lead into it very gently, try very hard not to be intrusive and begin with talking about the football. The Indian contingent spoke about the very strong personal relationships they had already in their teams, that they regularly discussed concerns about home life and that they would ask the question very directly.

Assumptions about cultural norms, behaviours and values can lead to misunderstandings and miscommunication. Avoid making assumptions; instead ask clarifying questions to better understand the other person's perspective.

Assessing

We have to make snap assessments about the urgency of a situation and whether to address it, and if so when, all the time. Where this really comes into play is when someone is using suicidal language. They may be indicating feeling worthless, or hopelessness for the future; they can't see the point in carrying on or even intimating that a weight has been lifted and they are sorting their affairs out.

- In the UK, men are three times more likely than women to die by suicide. In 2020, the male suicide rate was 16.9 per 100,000 population, while the female suicide rate was 5.2 per 100,000 population. However, more women are at risk of attempting suicide.

- Suicide is the leading cause of death for men under the age of 50 in the UK.
- The suicide rate for young people aged 15–24 has been increasing in recent years. In 2020, the suicide rate for this age group was 4.0 per 100,000 population, which is higher than the rate for any other age group. The young females age group, especially, has seen a significant increase[32].

Suicidal thoughts are common and not everyone who has thoughts will act on them. It may be that the best action for you to take is to engage in a direct conversation, addressing the issue head on. Asking someone if they are having thoughts of suicide does not make it more likely that they will act upon it – in fact it can be a relief to discuss it and therefore become a protective factor.

Ask directly – are you thinking about ending your life?

If they say yes, ask if they have thought about how and if they have spoken to anyone else about those thoughts. If someone has thought about plans or even preparation, that is an indicator that the risk is more urgent.

1. Connect: Show empathy and concern. It's important to actively listen to the person and ask open-ended questions to better understand their situation and what has changed recently that is causing them to feel this way.

2. Protect: If you believe that the person is at immediate risk of harm, it may be necessary to call emergency services or take other steps to ensure their safety.

3. Refer: This involves referring the person to appropriate resources and support. This may include providing information about mental health services, crisis hotlines, or other resources that can help the person get the support they need. Helping them to prioritise and put together an action plan to keep themselves safe is an excellent approach.

You could bring a course such as Suicide First Aid into your organisation if you are in a high-risk environment, recognising that not everyone who has thoughts of suicide has a mental health diagnosis. If your organisation is somewhere where your team are witnessing suicide or attempted suicide – for example railways, airports – you may consider a course which helps managers manage traumatic events.

Andrea Newton – Tutor, Survivor, Fighter

"Feeling completely overwhelmed by life and unable to keep going is a very scary and lonely place to be. It's difficult to think clearly, to see any other way out. People who are having these thoughts don't necessarily want to die, they simply want to find a way to make this pain end. Pain can be due to many issues – loss, relationship breakdown, financial challenges – and often just talking to someone honestly and openly without fear of ridicule or being made to feel 'stupid' for thinking that way, can be a massive help.

Being able to get your thoughts out of your head and into the open can feel incredibly helpful, like releasing the intensity of a pressure cooker and allowing it to settle. Sometimes just talking about it in a safe space with someone who is willing to listen, can be enough to help you see that actually, there **is** another way. Sometimes being signposted to help, someone acknowledging that your pain and distress is real, and sometimes simply just knowing that someone actually cares and that there are resources available to help can be enough. Never under-estimate the power of a single conversation in the fight against suicide."

Risk factors for suicide

1. Age: Suicide rates in the UK are highest among individuals aged 45–49 years, followed closely by those aged 50–54 years.
2. Gender: Men are three times more likely to die by suicide than women in the UK.
3. Ethnicity: In the UK, suicide rates are highest among individuals of White ethnicity, followed by those of Asian and Black ethnicities.
4. Marital status: Those who are divorced or separated are at a higher risk of suicide compared to those who are married or single.
5. Sexual orientation and gender identity: LGBTQ+ individuals, particularly transgender and non-binary

individuals, are at a higher risk of suicide than the general population.

6. Socioeconomic status: Individuals who are unemployed, experiencing financial difficulties, or living in poverty are at a higher risk of suicide.

7. History of mental health issues: Individuals with a history of mental illness, particularly depression, are at a higher risk of suicide.

8. Substance use: Substance abuse and dependence, particularly with alcohol and opioids, can increase the risk of suicide.

When considering risk factors for suicide, it is important to recognise the impact of intersectionality, as individuals who hold multiple marginalised identities may face additional barriers and risk factors that increase their risk for suicide.

For example, LGBTQ+ individuals who are also people of colour may experience discrimination and marginalisation based on both their race and sexual orientation/gender identity, which can compound the risk of suicide. Similarly, individuals who experience financial difficulties and also struggle with mental health issues may face additional challenges accessing resources and support, which can increase their risk of suicide.

Summary

- We can often easily spot the signs that someone is struggling, whether this is online or face-to-face, but sometimes this may first manifest as a performance issue or a physical health issue – remember physical and mental health are intrinsically linked.
- Managers should normalise asking whenever they have a concern – that means that it becomes less of a big, abnormal conversation.
- When it comes to a concern about someone considering taking their own life you should ask the question directly.

CHAPTER 12:

B FOR BE PRESENT

The greatest gift you can give someone is your presence.
Thich Nhat Hanh

Have you ever been to a therapist and found they say very little apart from 'Hmm'? That there is a lot of silence?

Whilst I found that particular 'silent' approach deeply frustrating sometimes, ultimately my grief counsellor (who I had for over a year due to the deaths of my mum, my dad and Rosie's OCD diagnosis all within the year) did very little aside from 'notice' certain things about my language or something I had said in a previous session and ask questions about those. It actually felt like a very useful exploration.

How does this help managers who, as we've already agreed, are not therapists?

You don't need to speak to be helpful

Often, we don't have to say very much to be helpful. Indeed, sometimes when we don't say very much but just allow the person to say everything they have to say, and show them that we have understood, that person may feel a sense of relief and then more able to tackle the next steps.

As we've seen, one of the reasons we avoid having these conversations is because we are afraid of not having answers or saying the wrong thing. However, if we approach these conversations in a spirit of curiosity, compassion and empathy; if we know that we don't have to have the answers there and then; if we think that our primary goal is to allow that person to be heard and **only then** move to looking at a plan, that can make it a less confronting conversation to begin.

Have you ever had a conversation about a problem which has been rolling round and round in your head and found that as you speak it, that problem seems less insurmountable? Just speaking out loud to someone non-judgemental can help us to shape our thoughts, especially if that person asks really insightful questions. They might say, "I see" or "That must be so difficult." Perhaps they might also summarise, "So what I hear you saying is… X, Y, Z – is that right?"

Carl Rogers, one of the founders of humanistic psychology and person-centred therapy, informs a lot of our approach to listening theory these days. He believed that individuals have the capacity within themselves to find their own solutions to their problems and challenges and that empathetic, non-judgemental conversations are a way of delivering these conditions.

Rogers also valued interpersonal connection and believed that true personal growth occurred through authentic communication and relationship-building.

It is true that a conversation in which vulnerability and true authentic communication is present seems to create a bond between people.

What humans often do though is think they are being more helpful by providing solutions (too quickly), playing devil's advocate, relating their own experience (in detail), or imposing their own view of the world on someone, for example, "Everything happens for a reason". Often this is down to wanting to be helpful, discomfort with someone else's pain or perhaps wanting to move the conversation along more quickly.

So, can't I say anything at all?

The famous phrase 'we have two ears and one mouth for a reason', doesn't mean we shouldn't use our mouths at all. We might want to normalise how difficult the situation is, to provide hope, to ask good questions, to ask if they have said everything they need to.

And of course, once they have said all they need to, we might suggest options and ideas for further support.

My friend Danny's boss

My friend Danny's dad recently died, and her boss left her the perfect voice note.

In essence it was, "I'm not going to call right now because you are with your family, but I just want you to know that I'm thinking about you. I don't know exactly what you are going through, because I haven't been there yet, but I know it is probably one of the hardest things you will ever go through. I know you too well not to know

> that you are being an amazing support to your mum right now, but I hope someone is taking care of you. Work can wait, take the next week off and let's see how you are and if you need more time at the end of that."
>
> My friend forwarded it to me with the words, "Best. Boss. Ever". What she got from that note was permission to not think about work, compassion, and a knowledge of her.

The temptation when someone is sharing something important, is to gabble, to fill the silence.

The better option is to take time to think, to ask better questions, to acknowledge what they have said, to allow them time to speak and then, yes of course, to co-create a plan.

The art of good questions

I was asked the best question I have ever been asked when I was in the middle of the mini burnout during my master's. My friend Lee, who is an all-round brilliant human being, witnessing my meltdown, asked me, "What is the most important thing for you right now?" Sobbing wildly, I said, "Getting a distinction in my next essay". He looked at me astounded and kindly (but laughing) said, "Is it, is it really? Is that really the most important thing for you right now?"

Ask question as much as possible but don't be afraid to say:

- Have you visited the doctor?
- Have you heard of our employee assistance programme?

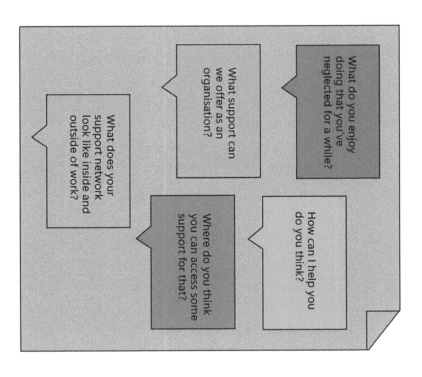

I suddenly remembered I had a family, my own health and my business – all of which came ahead of my master's. I had disappeared down a rabbit hole in which I was so overwhelmed I couldn't see what was important anymore. I was trying to run my own business whilst doing a master's and being a single parent. My perfectionism was in overdrive, made worse by insecurity and stress. Lee asking me this question twice enabled a light bulb moment for me.

Within a week I had put the master's on hold and taken two weeks off from the business to recalibrate.

Golden rules for listening

1. Pay attention: Give the person your full attention and don't look at your phone, your laptop, your dog, your child… It is the most irritating thing in the world if you are pouring your heart out to someone and they are distracted. Concentrate on what they are saying!
2. Use body language: Lean forward, use comfortable eye contact.
3. Notice your thoughts: Observe the thoughts in your head which are judging, solving, thinking about your own experience and compassionately bring yourself back to listening. You are only human!
4. Ask questions: Ask questions to clarify and show the person that you are listening. This also helps you understand better.

5. Don't interrupt: Allow the person to finish their thought before you respond. Then pause for a moment or two.

6. Reflect/summarise: You can show the person that you are listening by reflecting back to them. Repeat or summarise what they said to make sure that you understood it correctly.

7. Pause: Allow them time to say more and you time to think.

8. Acknowledge: Show them you have heard what they have said and that you understand. This can be small sounds or sentences.

9. Show respect: Respect what the person is saying, even if you don't agree. Don't be judgemental; try to keep an open mind.

10. Make time for individuals: Your primary role is to coach, develop and lead and the better you can do this, the more time you will eventually free up.

Summary

- It is counterintuitive for humans to really listen – we are problem-solving machines so we usually listen thinking about what our response should be.
- Developing self-compassion for our bad habits and noticing we are not really listening is key; we then need to bring ourselves back to attention.
- Our key task in the conversation is to acknowledge and understand.
- Showing that we understand may involve active listening techniques such as summarising, clarifying questions and using body language.

CHAPTER 13:

C FOR CO-CREATE A PLAN

Alone, we can do so little; together, we can do so much.

Helen Keller

Our quiz asks whether you "know what your company offers in terms of support for wellbeing issues and life struggles?" It is a good idea to have some of this knowledge in your back pocket but, we call this section 'Co-create' rather than create, because the best-case scenario is that the plan is created between the manager and the employee, not by the manager imposing it.

The more a realisation dawns with the person, and the more that they can take ownership for the next actions, the better the outcome. Like my sudden understanding of what I needed to do after my friend Lee asked me that question, "What is most important to you right now?" I didn't then need coaching through the next steps. I intrinsically just knew.

This may not always be the case though and people may not be aware of what options are open to them.

Don't feel under pressure to solve it all there and then either. Your plan might be as simple as, "Let's both go away and think about this – how we can support you and what support you might like and let's meet again tomorrow".

The likelihood is also that you may not be empowered to do everything you would like to offer that person – you may need to go and check, or suggest a follow up with occupational health or HR.

What kinds of things might we suggest?

Formal individual support

- Doctor: Has the person sought help from their doctor? If not, you should probably encourage this for a mental health issue. It may be related to a physical health issue which the doctor can uncover. If you are fortunate enough to have an online doctor available within your organisational wellbeing resources, you could signpost this facility.

- Employee Assistance Programme: Large organisations will typically all have one of these. They are generally poorly utilised because of the general scepticism many people may feel about accessing assistance at work for a mental health issue whilst worrying about the confidentiality of the service. They are also not well marketed within organisations. As a manager, you should highlight that any report that comes back to the organisation is completely anonymous. Inform the individual that they have access through the EAP to financial advisors, legal advisors, and, most importantly, counsellors. Most will offer at least six sessions and the support will be more or less immediate. Some will offer support for dependants too.

Informal individual support

- Friends and family: Asking who that person has in their support network, who do they talk to?
- General wellbeing measures: Asking how they are sleeping, eating, resting and exercising at the moment, and signposting to resources to support with these – you may have an intranet on which videos and books and articles will be available on this topic. You can also highlight authoritative resources such as the NHS, Mind and The Sleep Foundation.
- Local groups, specialist helplines.

Formal and informal organisational support

There are certain things you will have in your power to offer as their manager that you won't need to check in with any-one else about. These informal arrangements might include more one-to-one support from you on an aspect of their work, a buddy or mentoring scheme, time off (within their allocated leave), different working hours or place of work (if you operate a hybrid or flexible scheme). You might remove a project from them, or some aspect of their work temporarily, agree they come in late for a few days, or that they can attend therapy weekly in their work time.

Formal reasonable adjustments, however, may involve a deviation from standard policies or procedures, and to arrange this support you should get input and approval from higher levels of management and/or HR and make it clear you will need to ask for these, so you will need to share the information the employee has given you. These might need a more structured process, such as an assessment of the employee's needs, identification of potential adjustments, and discussion with the employee about the proposed adjustments.

There is more on your legal duties around reasonable adjustments in Chapter 14, but be aware your decisions in this area should be documented. You should make the adjustment time bound; for example, we review this in three weeks. If you don't do this, adjustments can run on and on and no longer serve the business or the team.

Summary

- Use clarifying questions to find possible points of next support or reasonable and practicable adjustments for the individual.
- Make your own suggestions too – for example, the Employee Assistance Programme or the doctor.
- Work together with the individual and don't overwhelm them with too much at once; a plan might simply be for both of you to think about what has been said and meet again the following day with some ideas.

CHAPTER 14:

D FOR YOUR DUTIES AS A MANAGER

People tend to forget their duties but remember their rights.
Indira Gandhi

What is a duty of care?

If you filled in the quiz at the beginning of this book, there was only one question relating to this very long chapter. "Do you understand your legal duties as a manager in line with the Equality Act 2010 and Health and Safety at Work etc Act 1974?"

Whilst this chapter takes you through some general duties and best practice, it also includes a glossary, designed to be dipped in and out of, which covers some of the increasingly common but trickier issues you may come across. You can use it as a reference when the time arises!

Important note: Where we refer to law and case law in this chapter it is UK focused. Please check your local regulations –

there are nuances in every country which are important. The first part of this chapter, the 'golden rules' are best-practice focused and can be widely applied; when we get to 'trickier issues' you should check your own local regulations as there are nuances everywhere and there are many changes afoot!

A duty of care refers to your legal and ethical responsibilities to do whatever is 'reasonably practicable' to ensure the health, safety and wellbeing of your employees. You have a duty to make sure that the working environment is safe, to protect your staff from discrimination and carry out risk assessments. Primarily, the duty to perform an organisational stress risk assessment is covered in a country's occupational health and safety laws.

The other primary piece of legislation relating to mental health is the Equality Act or equivalent in your country.

The Equality Act 2010 (EqA) in the UK covers disability discrimination (amongst other protected characteristics such as sex, age, race and religion). This is where, if you don't observe the rights that the EqA affords your employees and manage them accordingly, you may well end up defending a claim against you in the Employment Tribunal – especially if an employee ends up leaving, is dismissed or alleges they have been subjected to unlawful discrimination.

Under the EqA, employees who have a mental health condition **may be** considered to be suffering from a disability where they have a 'physical or mental impairment that has a substantial and long-term adverse effect on the ability to perform normal day-to-day tasks'. The criteria consider the nature, severity and length of the condition. Should an employee meet the legal definition, they are protected from discrimination and harassment if they are subjected to detrimental treatment because of their disability.

It is worth noting that some conditions and impairments are automatically protected under the EqA such as cancer, multiple sclerosis and a visual impairment, as are people with a progressive condition which gets worse over time, for example, Alzheimer's disease, motor neurone disease, muscular dystrophy and Parkinson's.

In the UK, unfair dismissal and discrimination cases are rising, as is their success and, unlike a claim for unfair dismissal, employees do not need to have worked for their employer for two years to bring a discrimination claim. There are also other exceptions to the two-year rule which include whistleblowing and requesting a statutory right (for example, maternity leave).

Check your local regulations but, in most countries, from an employment perspective we must therefore consider and be seen to consider (ensuring justifications for refusals) reasonable adjustments to accommodate and to avoid treating disabled employees less favourably because of their condition.

Reasonable adjustments for a mental ill health condition may comprise such things as:

- Changing the physical working environment, such as providing a quiet space, natural light, ergonomic equipment or changing location from home to workplace or vice versa

- Flexible working hours, breaks, or leave
- Additional support, such as providing mentoring, coaching, and/or counselling
- Taking a flexible approach to working hours, such as allowing part-time, compressed, or staggered hours
- Managing work volume, such as prioritising tasks, setting realistic deadlines, or delegating work
- Providing increased supervision, such as clarifying expectations, goals, and roles
- Increasing support from other members of staff, such as creating a buddy system, a peer support group, or a network of allies

Golden rules

Here are some golden rules for managing someone with a wellbeing issue. These are widely and globally applicable.

1. A prevention-first approach, tackling issues quickly when they arise. Be supportive but clear. Check in regularly with your team, ensuring that they have the time and resources to do their job appropriately. When issues do arise, agree how you can support the individual as an organisation but ensure that you are clear on review dates. At certain points in the process you may need to be clear about what they also need to do.

2. Considerations on confidentiality: Opening up about any health concerns can be tough, especially as mental health worries can be very personal. You should reassure the employee that you will not share anything they tell you, **unless there's a good reason to**. Note that you may indeed need to discuss with your HR business partner, occupational health provider or your own manager, and you should be clear about this in your conversation. Note, this is different to a peer-to-peer conversation where, unless there is a risk to life, you should always keep confidentiality.

3. On completing each conversation, write a short written summary for the individual about what you discussed and what was agreed, and email it to them. This creates clarity and shows the conversation took place. Ensure your language remains neutral when you write about the individual, in case you do end up in a tribunal and they apply for the disclosure, meaning they have rights to what has been written about them to support their claims.

4. If someone says they are struggling with a mental ill health issue, which may end up being considered a disability under the EqA or equivalent, you should demonstrate that you have considered reasonable adjustments and, where these are not practicable for you as an organisation, that you have communicated as to why they are not practicable. In parts of Europe, a company doctor will recommend these

adjustments. These adjustments should be time limited and reviewed.

5. Involve HR and their specialists and follow company
   policies and procedures.

6. When someone is off sick, stay in contact and always
   do a return-to-work interview.

Staying in contact

Acas guidance in the UK recommends that the employer
and employee stay in regular, organised contact when they
are off sick because of a mental health problem, particularly
if the employee is on long-term sickness absence. It can be
hard to stay in touch with someone struggling with a mental
ill health issue – maybe you are afraid of harassing them
– however, employees often benefit from keeping in touch.
Think about the consequence of **not** being in touch. They
will think you don't care or they are no longer needed. This
will lead to further disengagement.

Care should be taken to ensure that the level of communication is not overwhelming. They may need a week or two
with no communication from you when they go off sick but,
after that, agree with them their preferred method of contact
and the regularity. Unless the issue is partly to do with you,
as a manager you may be best placed to do this, but your HR
team can also take over.

Return-to-work interview

It's not a legal requirement to have a return-to-work meeting, but having a return-to-work meeting as soon as possible after an employee has returned is a good opportunity to:

- Make sure the employee is fit and ready to return to work and talk about any work updates or changes that have happened while they were off. You can also explain who did their work.
- See if they need any support and any adjustments.
- Agree on a plan for returning to work, if appropriate, for example a phased return to work.
- Talk about what they would like other employees to know about their absence and what they would like to keep confidential.

The employer might also:

- Look at any recommendations from the employee's doctor; and/or
- Consider a referral to a medical service such as occupational health.

Common mistakes made by UK employers
Pam Loch, employment lawyer

Being uninformed
Mistaken assumptions, for example, that an employee certified as unfit to work due to depression isn't well

enough to socialise with friends at the weekend, are made without understanding the impact of the condition on the person. The impact on one person will be different to the impact on another. Talk to your employee on a regular basis. The type of relationship that a manager builds with the employee is essential, and one that is based on trust will help the employee feel comfortable to discuss their condition and receive the support they need.

Not obtaining medical evidence

Medical evidence will help give you a better understanding of their condition and its impact. Consider referring them for an occupational health assessment and ensure that where reasonably practicable, any recommendations from occupational health are implemented. A common criticism of employers is their failure to consider and make reasonable adjustments to facilitate a return to work. This may be due to ignorance of the law or the benefits that can be achieved by making these adjustments.

Inadequate job descriptions

To ensure there is no confusion over what a job involves, it is essential to have a clear job description. It should clearly describe the specific duties and functions the employee will be expected to perform.

Lack of training

Managers should be given adequate training to equip them with the skills, knowledge and confidence to be able to have discussions with disabled employees about their condition and their needs without being concerned that they may make a mistake and or cause offence. They should know what the company's policies and procedures are and behave in a consistent way with all employees.

Managing increasingly common but trickier issues

The rest of this chapter references UK-specific law but, as these issues affect employees worldwide, there are general principles that can be understood and investigated under the laws and jurisdiction of your own country.

Performance managing someone with a mental health issue

Poor mental health can affect performance and, as we covered in Chapter 11: A for Awareness, sometimes you will only be aware that the individual is struggling when their performance dips.

When managing employees with mental ill health issues, you still should follow performance management procedures. You should consider what support should be given sooner, but you can still engage in your normal processes, always erring on the side of caution and considering if the EqA applies, particularly where an employee declares that they are stressed or perhaps has a formal diagnosis of anxiety or has had prior issues with panic attacks.

When mental ill health issues play a role, managers should consider adjusting processes to ensure there are no disadvantages to the employee. For instance, something we often see is the employee having a friend or family member attend meetings. It's sensible to consider if you need a medical opinion to make sure any adjustments to the process are fair and that the right support is in place.

You may want to understand what support they already have in place – for example, do they already have a therapist they trust, or can you signpost them to one? Some organisations use their Employee Assistance Programme for this, some will use a paid for counsellor and others will reimburse expenses for therapy. Look at what support your organisation can supply – either formal or informal. They may need some time off, perhaps a short-term adjustment to hours or place of work or even type of work. If a formal reasonable adjustment is needed, you should make sure that this is time limited and put in place with support from your HR team.

A fair performance management procedure will involve:

- Consultation with the employee
- Medical investigation often with input from a doctor or occupational health
- Considering re-deployment
- Considering and making reasonable adjustments

Disability

Everyone has an equal right to employment and the benefits of employing disabled people include:

- Improved corporate culture, creating a more diverse and inclusive workplace, which can lead to a range

of benefits, including increased creativity and
innovation, better problem-solving, and improved
decision-making

- Access to a wider talent pool
- Lower employee turnover
- Improved customer service (a greater understanding
of diverse needs and experiences)
- Positive impact on society
- Enhanced reputation

Be aware that in the UK, employees are not required to
disclose their disability to their employer, and employers are
not allowed to ask job candidates or employees about their
health or disability status during the recruitment process or
in the workplace.

However, many employers will ask if the applicant needs
adjustments in the application form or when they are invited to interview, and if they are going to ask for reasonable
adjustments, they will need to declare that they are disabled.

If an employee requires reasonable adjustments to perform their job due to a disability, they need to ensure that
their employer knows they have a disability so that the company can provide them with the necessary support. These
should be tailored to their individual needs – don't make
assumptions about what they are – often the employee will
know best. The Employer's Occupational Health provider
will also be able to support here.

The employer does not have to change the basic nature of
the job, particularly if this means that there would be no oth-

er job for them to perform. Also, what is reasonable depends on each situation. The employer should discuss with the employee whether the adjustment will remove or reduce the disadvantage, considering other factors such as whether the adjustment is practical and affordable to make, and whether it could harm the health and safety of others. There is a government initiative, the Access to Work scheme, which provides support to disabled people and those with health conditions to enable them to work. The employee needs to apply for the support and can do so at https://www.gov.uk/access-to-work.

Financial challenges

Increasing numbers within your team may be struggling with their finances, and the impact of worrying about money can increase stress enormously. The temptation for those affected can be to ignore the problem but it is so important to control what can be controlled when it comes to finances.

Your Employee Assistance Programme should provide money advice, but you can also proactively educate by providing a course or access to a financial advisor. You can offer perks that help employees with common money worries, such as flexible working hours, salary advances, loans, savings schemes, childcare vouchers or discounts. You should of course lobby to ensure fair salaries and be mindful of expenses, such as travel costs, uniforms or equipment, that may put a strain on employees' budgets. For more detailed information, check out the Money Charity, in the further resources at the end of this book.

Neurodiversity

Between 15 and 20 percent of us have a neurodiversity. Common types are dyslexia, dyspraxia, ADHD and autism spectrum disorder.

Awareness and education are the first part of the puzzle. Currently there is a great deal of interest in the neurodiversity awareness courses we run. Organisations are becoming aware of the impact of not understanding this area and that there may be significant benefits from embracing it.

Concentrating less on fit, and more on the actual strengths and competencies required for a role, is key to managing in this area, because often issues at work for those with a neurodiversity are nothing to do with capability and all to do with not fitting the mould of a good employee.

Those with dyslexia are often highly creative and offer out-of-the-box thinking, which can be incredibly useful in the competitive environment we operate in today. Famously, over 50 percent of NASA's workforce are dyslexic. Those with autism may have exceptional mathematical skills and sustained powers of concentration.

People with neurodiverse conditions could meet the legal definition of disability as defined in the EqA, however they are not automatically deemed as having a disability so they still must meet the requirements set out in the EqA. Neurodiverse conditions are sometimes categorised as having special needs, learning difficulties or disorders. Some individuals identify with these labels and others do not. All neurodiverse people have individual needs, and many will require reasonable adjustments at work.

Menopause

As women over 50 are the fastest growing demographic in the workplace, a subject which was spoken little about and not understood even by those going through it, is fast becoming a significant issue to understand and manage.

Key symptoms which may impact on the workplace are:

- Changes to cognitive function which may mean it is harder to focus on tasks and remember/work out important details
- Fatigue, a lack of energy, insomnia
- Hot flashes, sweating and flooding
- Mood swings and irritability

As a manager you probably don't want to say (As I once did!!), "Do you think you are menopausal?" (Sorry!)

Instead, focus on some of the behaviours you have noticed such as tiredness or irritability. Ask if there is anything you can help with, or whether they've sought support, for example, from their doctor.

The symptoms of the menopause can be a disability if the symptoms meet the legal test, that is, an impairment which is long lasting and has a substantial adverse effect on an employee's ability to carry out day-to-day activities – meaning reasonable adjustments must be made.

The list of reasonable adjustments for menopausal women might include:

- Flexible working arrangements
- Access to a private, cool room
- Adjusting uniform requirements
- Access to a fan or personal cooling device
- Offering frequent breaks
- Access to toilets to deal with flooding which can be difficult and embarrassing
- Creating easy-to-follow guides for new systems and processes can be a helpful reasonable adjustment for menopausal women in the workplace. By providing clear, step-by-step instructions, employers can help menopausal women navigate new systems or processes without feeling overwhelmed or stressed.
- Providing training for managers and colleagues on the impact of menopause can help create a supportive and understanding workplace culture.

Bereavement

If you have ever been bereaved, you will know that everyone processes loss in a different way and for some it can be an incredibly hard time. Allowing people time, not only to make arrangements for loved ones but to process the loss, is important, whilst being patient and supportive.

In some cases, a bereavement leads to ordinary symptoms of grief which would not be a disability. In others they may lead to something more profound which is, or develops into, an impairment over time and one that can be long lasting. Regardless of whether or not bereaved employees satisfy the definition of a disability, under EqA you should offer extra support as far as you are able, such as bereavement counselling or other forms of assistance. Offer flexible working hours and/or the option for the employee to work from home. Above all, accept that the grieving process takes time and being supportive of the employee during this difficult time can make a significant difference.

Terminal illness

For many people, a diagnosis of terminal illness does not mean immediately having to give up on normal activities although they are likely to be considered as having a deemed disability under EqA. Work is an important part of all our lives, and the individual's opportunity to continue contributing within the workplace and socialising with work colleagues may be a positive part of coming to terms with the diagnosis, and being able to enjoy their remaining life to its full. It also crucially helps provide financial security for themselves and their loved ones.

Don't make your processes and procedures so rigid that when an employee with a terminal illness approaches you, you can't discuss what they would like at this time. Lighter duties? Flexible work? More time off? Ability to attend appointments as needed?

Ideally managers should be able to signpost affected employees to advisers on benefits and financial options available, as well as support and advice from an Employee Assistance Programme and occupational health service.

You need to have the facts and present those clearly – for example, what does your sick pay allow for? Discuss the impact of early ill-health retirement and any pension provision with the employee so that they can plan appropriately. There may be other benefits available that should be highlighted such as critical illness cover and death-in-service benefit.

Do involve your HR team in this conversation but good workplaces should ask the employee what they would like, explain the impact of their decisions but be as flexible as possible.

Care of dependants

An employee's dependants can include:

- their husband, wife, civil partner or partner
- their child
- their parent
- a person who lives in their household (not tenants, lodgers or employees)
- a person who relies on them, such as an elderly neighbour

Employees are entitled to emergency leave to care for dependants and is usually unpaid.

The law does not say how much time an employee can take off, or how many occasions. It just says the amount should be 'reasonable' as it depends on the situation. The employer should be as flexible as they can be, depending on the employee's circumstances. How much time they need will depend on what has happened, but as an employer you are only required by law to pay in certain circumstances – for example, whilst care is being arranged, or for emergency appointments. Good organisations though will look at perhaps a mix of paid and unpaid leave.

There is also the right to two weeks' leave and statutory bereavement pay if you lose a child under the age of 18. The Carer's Leave Act 2023 also gives employees who care for a friend or relative the opportunity to take one week's unpaid leave additionally each year.

Transgender/transitioning

This is currently a hugely present issue and managers need to be aware of it because it's important to understand the current legal protections in place, at time of publication in 2023. The EqA provides that gender reassignment is identified as a protected characteristic. This is reiterated in the Equality and Human Rights Commission Statutory of Code of Conduct, which was last updated in September 2015. The EqA affords protection against discrimination based on gender reassignment, which includes those people who are proposing to undergo, are undergoing, or have undergone a process or part of a process for the purpose of reassigning their gender by changing physiological or other attributes of gender. This means it is unlawful to discriminate against someone on the basis of their transgender status, both when employing transgender workers and during the course of a person's employment.

This protection is extended to practical measures, such as dress codes and toilet facilities, as well as harassment and discrimination within the workplace.

This is wholly separate from the Gender Recognition Act 2004, which allows transgender people to gain legal recognition. Anyone who holds a certificate must be treated according to their stated gender; however, it goes without saying that managers should use the employee's preferred name and pronouns, even if they have not legally changed their name or gender. If you are unsure, ask the employee directly how they prefer to be addressed.

Summary

- As a manager, your duty is to follow best-practice guidance, which is applicable wherever you are in the world, in dealing with any wellbeing issues in your team.
- Trickier issues are becoming increasingly common and advice on concerns such as menopause, performance issues, bereavement and terminal illness are included in this chapter. Note these specific issues are written with UK law in mind.
- Reasonable adjustments are detailed for specific concerns and suggestions are offered for how these also may apply to a mental ill health issue.

CONCLUSION:

HOW GOOD MANAGERS CAN HELP HUMANITY

In this book we have seen that we live in uncertain times and many of us are struggling. We have seen that leaders and managers are the drivers of wellbeing in an organisation and that many are not trained to create a team which thrives, nor are they trained to have conversations with those who are struggling.

Hopefully you took our quiz at the beginning of the book – do take it again in a few weeks' time and see if you have managed to integrate any lessons from *I'm a boss, not a shrink*. If you would like a safe space in which to practise this conversation, contact us and we will bring our training course to you and use our actors for you to practise with (not role play by the way – forum theatre!)

I'm increasingly convinced that being a good manager has a lot in common with just being a good human. I know in the places where I have failed as a manager not only impacted me as a human, but also showed me some hidden part of myself which I hadn't acknowledged or yet understood, and which drove me towards less-than-optimal behaviours.

In these disruptive, chaotic times we live in, we need to evolve as humans, growing in empathy, understanding, and effective communication skills. Manager training also needs to evolve in terms of greater focus on self-awareness, self-regulation, empathy and emotional intelligence. Perhaps over time, we will hire managers to manage instead of to continue doing so much of the day job too.

Being a good manager and being a good human both involve being a leader. A good manager needs to set a positive example for their team members to follow, just as a good human needs to set a positive example for those around them.

My invitation to you is to embark on a journey of self-awareness, in the full knowledge that you are human and will never be 'fixed'. This journey will lead you to a calmer, more self-accepting place, where you can be of true service to your team.

Preferred management models differ around the world and even within companies. However, more recent ideas emphasise the importance of serving others, rather than being served. Leaders who follow this model prioritise the needs of their employees or team members and seek to support and empower them to achieve their goals.

There is no doubt also that being a manager is very tough these days. It's a far cry from those simple days when we could just tell people what we wanted from them, didn't have to watch our words so carefully and our home life was more simple.

In fact, around half of managers wish someone had warned them not to take their current job (57 percent) and also say it's likely they'll quit their job within the next 12 months because they're experiencing too much work-related stress (46 percent)[33].

But if you retain anything from this book, then let it be the desire to understand yourself and your own drivers better, to learn to listen actively and non-judgementally and when you get it wrong, which you inevitably will, clean it up and forgive yourself.

You're only human after all.

GLOSSARY

Employee Assistance Programmes

An Employee Assistance Programme (EAP) is a type of workplace service that provides advice and support for employees. EAPs typically provide employees with access to confidential counselling and support services, such as short-term counselling, stress management and legal advice. They may also provide services such as financial planning and education, career counselling and referral services.

Equality Act (2010)

The Equality Act 2010 protects people with disabilities from discrimination in the workplace and in wider society. It states that employers must make reasonable adjustments to make sure disabled people are not at a substantial disadvantage when compared to their non-disabled peers. It also requires employers to make sure that disabled people have access to employment opportunities, goods, services and premises. In addition, the Act prohibits employers from discriminating against disabled people in recruitment, promotion and other aspects of employment.

ISO 45003

ISO 45003 is a standard with the goal of providing guidance on how to manage the mental health of employees in the workplace. The standard was published in 2021 and is titled "Occupational health and safety management – Psychological health and safety at work – Guidelines for managing psychosocial risks."

The standard recognises that mental health is a critical component of overall health and wellbeing, and that it can be impacted by work-related factors such as workload, job demands, organisational culture and interpersonal relationships. The standard aims to provide managers with practical guidance on how to identify, assess and manage these psychosocial risks in order to promote a positive and healthy work environment.

Some of the key elements of ISO 45003 include:

- Understanding the principles of psychological health and safety at work
- Identifying psychosocial risks in the workplace
- Assessing the severity of those risks and their potential impact on employees
- Implementing measures to control and manage those risks
- Monitoring and evaluating the effectiveness of those measures
- Encouraging participation and collaboration between management and employees in the management of psychosocial risks

Overall, ISO 45003 is intended to provide organisations with a framework for managing the mental health of their employees in a proactive and systematic way, ultimately with the goal of promoting a positive and healthy work environment that supports the wellbeing of all employees.

Occupational Health Providers

An occupational health provider is someone who provides health care services to people in the workplace. Occupational health providers can include doctors, nurses, physical therapists and other medical professionals. They specialise in diagnosing and treating workplace-related health issues, such as musculoskeletal disorders, repetitive strain injuries and workplace stress. They can also provide advice and guidance on ergonomic design and work practices, as well as advice on the implementation of health and safety policies.

Psychological safety

Psychological safety is a shared belief held by members of a team that the team is safe for interpersonal risk-taking. It's a sense of confidence that the team will not embarrass, reject or punish someone for speaking up, asking questions, or offering ideas. Psychological safety is essential for team effectiveness, innovation and learning.

Stress risk assessment (HSE)

The Health and Safety at Work etc Act 1974 places a legal obligation on employers to ensure the health, safety and welfare of their employees, including taking steps to prevent harm to employees' mental health due to work-related stress.

An organisational stress risk assessment is required by The Health and Safety at Work etc Act 1974 and it is an evaluation of the potential risks posed by workplace stress. It is used to identify potential hazards, assess the risk they pose, and create a plan to reduce or eliminate those risks. The assessment typically includes an evaluation of the working environment, job duties and responsibilities, support from managers and resources. The management standards from HSE can support here.

REFERENCES

Prologue

1   "Improving Line Management", TUC, 9 May, 2019,
    https://www.tuc.org.uk/research-analysis/reports/
    improving-line-management?page=1

Introduction

2   "Investigation of the links between psychological
    ill health, stress and safety", The Keil Centre
    for the Health and Safety Executive, 2006,
    https://healthyworkcompany.com/wp-content/
    uploads/2023/06/rr488.pdf

3   Mulder, S, Rooy, D de, "Pilot Mental Health,
    Negative Life Events, and Improving Safety with
    Peer Support and a Just Culture", Jan 2018, https://
    pubmed.ncbi.nlm.nih.gov/29233243/

4   Johnson, S, "Suicide still treated as a crime in at
    least 20 countries, report finds", The Guardian, 9
    Sep 2021 https://www.theguardian.com/global-
    development/2021/sep/09/suicide-still-treated-as-a-
    in-at-least-20-countries-report-finds

Chapter 1

5   Shah, K, Tomlinson, D, "Work experiences: Changes in the subjective experience of work, The Economy 2030 Inquiry", May 2021

6   "Single Parents, Facts and figures", Gingerbread, https://www.gingerbread.org.uk/our-work/policy-and-campaigns/research-publications/statistics/

7   "COVID-19 pandemic triggers 25% increase in prevalence of anxiety and depression worldwide", World Health Organization, February 2022, https://www.who.int/news/item/02-03-2022-covid-19-pandemic-triggers-25-increase-in-prevalence-of-anxiety-and-depression-worldwide

Chapter 2

8   https://www.cdc.gov/nchs/products/databriefs/db377.htm

9   "COVID-19 pandemic triggers 25% increase in prevalence of anxiety and depression worldwide", World Health Organization, February 2022, https://www.who.int/news/item/02-03-2022-covid-19-pandemic-triggers-25-increase-in-prevalence-of-anxiety-and-depression-worldwide

10   Hari, Johann. (2018). *Lost Connections: Why You're Depressed and How to Find Hope*. London: Bloomsbury

11   Ibbetson, C, "How many people don't have a best friend", September 2019, https://yougov.co.uk/topics/society/articles-reports/2019/09/25/quarter-britons-dont-have-best-friend

12   Buettner, Dan. (2008). *The Blue Zones: Lessons for Living Longer From the People Who've Lived the Longest*. Washington, DC: National Geographic Society

13   Criado Perez, C, (2019). Invisible women: Data bias in a world designed for men, London: Chatto & Windus

14   Garcia-Alonso, J, Krentz, M, Lovich, D, Quickenden, D, "Lightening the mental load that holds women back" Boston Consulting Group, April 2019, https://www.bcg.com/publications/2019/lightening-mental-load-holds-women-back

15   Haidt, Jonathan. (2012). *The Righteous Mind: Why Good People are Divided by Politics and Religion*. New York, NY: Vintage

16   Rutledge, Robb, 'Lowering expectations can increase happiness", May 2021, https://www.ucl.ac.uk/news/headlines/2021/may/lowering-expectations-can-increase-happiness

Chapter 3

17   Gallup, State of the global workplace, 2022 report, https://www.gallup.com/workplace/349484/state-of-the-global-workplace-2022-report.aspx

18   Pym, H, "Big rise in long-term sick hitting UK workforce", Feb 2023, https://www.bbc.co.uk/news/health-64703051

19   "Sickness absence in the UK labour market 2021", https://www.ons.gov.uk/employmentandlabourmarket/peopleinwork/labourproductivity/articles/sicknessabsenceinthelabourmarket/2021

20   https://healthyworkcompany.com/policy-practice-for-organisational-wellbeing/

21   "Tackling work-related stress using the Management Standards approach", March 2019, https://www.hse.gov.uk/pubns/wbk01.htm

22   "Occupational health and safety management. Psychological health and safety at work. Guidelines for managing psychosocial risks", June 2021 https://knowledge.bsigroup.com/products/occupational-health-and-safety-management-psychological-health-and-safety-at-work-guidelines-for-managing-psychosocial-risks/rd?awc=3911_1660060856_77bf71716890544040470035d-c29df2a

Chapter 4

23   "Thriving at Work: a review of mental health and employers" 26 October 2017, https://www.gov.uk/government/publications/thriving-at-work-a-review-of-mental-health-and-employers

Chapter 5

24   Yerkes, R M, Dodson, J D, (1908). "The relationship of strength of stimulus to rapidity of habit formation", Journal of Comparative Neurology and Psychology, vol 18, pp 459–482

Chapter 6

25   Beck, R, Harter, J, "Managers Account for 70% of Variance in Employee Engagement", 21 April, 2015, https://news.gallup.com/businessjournal/182792/managers-account-variance-employee-engagement.aspx

26   "Mental Health at Work: Managers and Money", https://www.ukg.com/resources/article/mental-health-work-managers-and-money

27   Candid Camera, Elevator conformity experiment https://www.facebook.com/watch/?v=307794423346316

Chapter 7

28   Johnson, Robert. (1991). *Owning Your Own Shadow: Understanding the Dark Side of the Psyche*. NewYork, NY: HarperOne

29   Neff, Kristen. (2011). *Self-Compassion: Stop Beating Yourself Up and Leave Insecurity Behind*. New York, NY: HarperCollins

30   Frost Multidimensional Perfectionism Scale (FMPS)
      https://novopsych.com.au/assessments/formulation/
      frost-multidimensional-perfectionism-scale-fmps/

Chapter 8

31   Csikszentmihalyi, Mihaly. (1990). *Flow: The
      Psychology of Optimal Experience.* New York, NY:
      Harper and Row Publishers

Chapter 11

32   "Suicides in England and Wales: 2021 registrations",
      Office for National Statistics, Census 2021, https://
      www.ons.gov.uk/peoplepopulationandcommunity/
      birthsdeathsandmarriages/deaths/bulletins/
      suicidesintheunitedkingdom/2021registrations

Conclusion

33   "Mental Health at Work, Managers and
      Money", https://www.ukg.com/resources/
      article/mental-health-work-managers-and-
      money?ms=4357.142857142857

RESOURCES

FURTHER READING

Buettner, Dan. (2008). *The Blue Zones: Lessons for Living Longer From the People Who've Lived the Longest.* Washington, DC: National Geographic Society

Csikszentmihalyi, Mihaly. (1990). *Flow: The Psychology of Optimal Experience.* New York, NY: Harper and Row Publishers

Edmondson, Amy. (2018). *The Fearless Organization: Creating Psychological Safety in the Workplace for Learning, Innovation, and Growth.* Hoboken, NJ: John Wiley & Sons

Farrell, William. (1990). *Why Men Are The Way They Are.* New York, NY: Berkley Books

Haidt, Jonathan. (2012). *The Righteous Mind: Why Good People are Divided by Politics and Religion.* New York, NY: Vintage

Hari, Johann. (2018). *Lost Connections: Why You're Depressed and How to Find Hope.* London: Bloomsbury

Johnson, Robert. (1991). *Owning Your Own Shadow: Understanding the Dark Side of the Psyche.* NewYork, NY: HarperOne

Lyubomirsky, Sonja. (2007). *The How of Happiness: A Scientific Approach to Getting the Life You Want.* New York, NY: Penguin Press

Murphy, Kate. (2020). *You're Not Listening: What You're Missing and Why it Matters.* New York, NY: Celadon Books

Meyer, Erin. (2014). *The Culture Map: Breaking Through the Invisible Boundaries of Global Business.* New York, NY: PublicAffairs

Neff, Kristen. (2011). *Self-Compassion: Stop Beating Yourself Up and Leave Insecurity Behind.* New York, NY: HarperCollins

Rogers, C R, Farson, R E. (1957). *Active Listening.* Homewood, IL: R D Irwin, Inc

Santos, Dr Laurie. (2020). *The Science of Well-Being.* New Haven, CT: Yale University Press

Seligman, Martin. 2002. *Authentic Happiness: Using the New Positive Psychology to Realize your Potential for Lasting Fulfillment.* New York, NY: Free Press

Seligman, Martin. (2011). *Flourish: A Visionary New Understanding of Happiness and Well-being.* New York, NY: Free Press

van der Kolk, Bessel. (2014). *The Body Keeps the Score: Brain, Mind, and Body in the Healing of Trauma.* New York, NY: Viking van Dernoot Lipsky, Laura. (2018). *The Age of Overwhelm: Strategies for the Long Haul.* Oakland, CA: Berrett-Koehler Publishers

Wong, Dr Paul (2011). *"Positive psychology 2.0: Towards a balanced interactive model of the good life".* http://www.drpaulwong.com/positive-psychology-2-0-towards-a-balanced-interactive-model-of-the-good-life/

FURTHER SUPPORT

Mental illness (UK-based support)

NHS: Every Mind Matters: https://www.nhs.uk/oneyou/every-mind-matters/

Mind: https://www.mind.org.uk/

Rethink Mental Illness: https://www.rethink.org/

Samaritans: https://www.samaritans.org/

Mental Health Foundation: https://www.mentalhealth.org.uk/

Managing your own wellbeing (UK-based support)

NHS: Live Well: https://www.nhs.uk/live-well/

British Nutrition Foundation: https://www.nutrition.org.uk/

Sleep Foundation: https://www.sleepfoundation.org/

The Mental Health Foundation – How to Look After Your Mental Health Using Exercise: https://www.mental-health.org.uk/publications/how-to-using-exercise

The Body Coach TV: https://www.youtube.com/channel/UCAxW1XT0iEJo0TYlRfn6rYQ

National Institute for Health and Care Excellence (NICE). (2015). Menopause: diagnosis and management. Clinical guideline [CG23]. https://www.nice.org.uk/guidance/ng23

For managers and organisations

Healthy Work Company for training and strategy support with wellbeing: https://www.healthyworkcompany.com/

Loch Associates for legal employment support – individually or for your organisation: https://www.lochassociates.co.uk/

Access to Work scheme: https://www.gov.uk/access-to-work

Mind Wellness Action Plans: https://www.mind.org.uk/workplace/mental-health-at-work/wellness-action-plan-sign-up/

Robertson Cooper: https://robertsoncooper.com/

Gallup: https://www.gallup.com/home.aspx

Business in the Community (BITC) Workwell: https://www.bitc.org.uk/the-wellbeing-workwell-model/

McKinsey & Company – Health: https://www.mckinsey.com/industries/healthcare-systems-and-services/our-insights

Engaging overview of ISO45003: https://vimeo.com/571580356

Conformity experiment: https://www.facebook.com/watch/?ref=search&v=790603841401707

Unison report on dealing with terminal illness: https://www.unison.org.uk/content/uploads/2019/03/Terminal-illness-03-2019.pdf

The Money Charity – Financial wellbeing and Financial education: https://themoneycharity.org.uk/

ACKNOWLEDGEMENTS

I was unprepared for the lonely roller coaster ride which running your own business can be.

I thought having run other people's businesses prepared me perfectly. Yes, I knew a thing or two, but I wasn't prepared for the stress of generating my own income from scratch every month, nor for how life events – elderly and dying parents, mini-burnouts, my daughter's OCD – would prevent me from working from time to time.

I feel very grateful to have had wonderful parents who were so proud of me and my beautiful sis who has taken their mantle since they died, together with her lovely husband and two children. My daughter, Rosie, who is the best companion ever, never lets me get too big for my boots. Neither does my ex-husband, Richard with whom I remain great friends.

But I have been extremely lucky with my customers.

From day one I have been trusted to try new things in the context of extremely supportive relationships – where in almost all cases, I feel less of a supplier and more of a friend.

This isn't, by any means, a comprehensive list of our customers at all, but I would particularly like to thank some of those who supported me early on and those whom I still look to for inspiration (and their business!).

Ruth Denyer, formerly ITV and now Netflix, along with Ruth Gallagher (at Heathrow at the time) were my first two customers. Ruth Denyer continues to upgrade my education and enhance my life with her smiles every time I see her. Lucy Haywood gave us our first multi-training order at MAN Truck & Bus and continues to involve me in talks at Bayer. John Green (was at Laing O'Rourke and now at NEOM) gave me an enormous group to train a few months in and then proceeded to ask me during COVID to run a webinar for thousands in French and English! Natasha Scoggins at Eurostar asked me to do a stress risk assessment in the middle of manager training before anyone was doing them really. Gnosoulla Tsioupra-Lewis as well as uncovering my inner feminist(!) allowed me to try out my first talks at UBM and then hired me when she moved to the Telegraph, where I still work closely with brilliant Becky Holland.

Simon Bown of KeolisAmey Docklands together with Brad Pettman of London Array are just two of the best humans, and have more faith in me than I have in myself. I am grateful that Kirsty Duncan and Kath Beard at ITV are some of the few clients who realise that this training needs to be run consistently for new starters and promotions so book us regularly throughout the year. First Margo Mosley (a super friend), then David Revitt and Ian Wratten at Vertex Pharmaceuticals continue to allow me to work consistently with them. Ditto with Emma Meenan and

Sam Cartwright at Luton Airport. At Heathrow I have been involved in initiatives with Sharon Smith and Amanda Owen but was privileged to provide support work to Becky Corris on their wellbeing strategy. I've been particularly proud of the "Train the Trainer" programmes we have run at Mace with Kerrie Smith and Dr Judith Grant (also a great friend); CVS with Claire Dennison and Adele Wood and a multilingual, multinational programme at Givaudan with John Pares.

I've also had personal help and supportive conversations with far too many people to count (many also highlighted above as customers!) but here are a few: Dr Tim Marsh (thank you for so much), Victoria Brookbank, Keith Hole, Louise Hosking, Jonathan Gawthrop, James Pomeroy, Shirley Parsons, Sheila Pantry, Peter Kelly, Keith Shaw, Keith Scott, Christian Hopper, Ian Cooke, Sarah Wilson, Phillip Pearson, Dave Hamilton, Margaret Finn, Charlie Alberts, Stacy Thompson, Lou Kiwanuka, Liz Shuttleworth, Jerry Flechais, Maeve O'Loughlin, Karl Simons, Clive Johnson, the always fun David Bishop, new friend Diane Chadwick-Jones. Special thanks to Fiona Coffey for her insightful tea and tarot!

And then there are those who have supported me to deliver. Anna Keen at Acre gave me the self-belief and helped bring my first customers on board. At Informa (my old employer) I am grateful for the ongoing support from Charlotte Geoghegan, Chris Edwards, Ian Hart, Mark Glover. Thank you to Highfield for trusting me to co-create their mental health qualifications. Also to our brilliant trainers – David Whiting,

Lis Cashin, Andrea Newton, Sam Langford, Sarah Wilsher, Alastair Clamp and our theatre director, Eliot Giuralarocca. In the background at HWC, there have been multiple helpers – Pam Loch, our HR Employment Advisor, Coconut Marketing, Mrs K Designs, Richard Pond marketing, Emily Cleary, Sylvia Fielding, Gemma da Silva, Richard  Bowman, CEM bookkeeping (oh and of course my therapist Stephanie Bushell and canine support Rocky the dog).

I want to also highlight some people I have worked with who have made an impact. Adrian Newton at UBM, gave me the opportunity to turn Barbour EHS around and then also hired me for training when he went to the *New Scientist*. Simon Mills, who although I have given him the moniker of #bestboss still hasn't hired me at ExCeL! To Teresa Higgins and all the team at Barbour EHS and especially to Victoria Sadler who understands me so well and laughs at the good and bad of me.

This book literally wouldn't exist without the slave driver of a coach – Will Steel, who also came up with the title, nor without the patience of my editor, Erin Chamberlain.

Like many people during COVID I decided going forward that I would be more mindful about who I spend my time with, which includes some sadly very spread-out close friends…Danny Green, Mike Waplington, Penni Gillen, Jane Golby, Patricia Charles (known since I was four), Sarah Whelan, Susan Miles, Jacques Verdier (et la famille Verdier), John Shardlow, Nat Cotterill, Jo Tunmer, Sophia and Andy Steeden, Rachel Risley. Those who I love and wish I could see more overseas but who are always cheering me on including Derek Chambers, Dr Fiona Martin, the Chickpeas (Rachel and Andy), Katie Blake, Chantal, Cheesy Leas, Suzanne Parsons, the Hegartys, Joe Drumgoole (thank you for all the steak!). Family-wise we are a bit depleted now, but my cousins and their partners – Russ, Ade and Kev (two of whom are in health and safety!), the Solas, my one remaining Aunty (Eileen) and my mother-outlaw, Pat.

Particular love to those who have had to rescue me in the very recent past – Lee Silver, Siobhan Connolly Hogan, Urmi Dutta Roy, Marisol Navarro, Sally Kemp (yes you are all my friends too, but you have special gifts when it comes to supporting la Beach!)

Last but by no means least, for the first four years of the wild ride which has been HWC, it was a core team: me, Lauren Applebey and Natasha Seremenho (Tash).

We did some amazing things together and saw each other through deaths, illnesses, pregnancies and piles. Tash rescued me when my mum died and got me to her house on the Algarve (where she now sells second homes!). It was a special time and I am so grateful we are still friends in spite of all the mistakes I made. Six years in, having learnt so much, I have the calm and organised Claire Young as my right-hand person and it finally feels like the Flying Fish children's ride at Thorpe Park rather than the Stealth roller coaster.

ABOUT THE AUTHOR

Heather **Beach** is founder of Healthy Work Company and of Women in Health and Safety and single mum to Rosie. An ex-Director for a global company, where she ran their health and safety businesses publishing magazines, running conferences and information services, she now runs Healthy Work Company working with businesses such as ITV, Kuehne and Nagel, KAD, Mace, Eurostar, the Telegraph, Vertex, Game and Luton Airport to support wellbeing strategy and wellbeing training. She has a particular focus on manager training in good wellbeing conversations because she knows the difference a good manager can make.

With post graduate certificates in Applied Positive Psychology and Relational Organisation Gestalt, she is also certified in Implementation of BS45001 and was voted in the top ten most influential people in health and safety in the UK for the third year running in 2021. Heather has been a featured expert on TV and in national press in the conversation about mental health during lockdown.

As a small business owner, she isn't perfect, but tries very hard to practise what she preaches.

Milton Keynes UK
Ingram Content Group UK Ltd.
UKHW020714101123
432310UK00011B/77